Landing On Your Feet

Landing On Your Feet

P.19 E.A.R.N.

The Canadian Guide to Surviving, Coping, and Prospering from Job Loss

Mara Brown

McGraw-Hill Ryerson
Toronto   Montreal

Landing On Your Feet
The Canadian Guide to Surviving, Coping, and
Prospering from Job Loss

Copyright © 1992 by Mara Brown

First published in 1992 by
McGraw-Hill Ryerson Limited
300 Water Street
Whitby, Ontario, Canada
L1N 9B6

1 2 3 4 5 6 7 8 9 0 W 1 0 9 8 7 6 5 4 3 2

Canadian Cataloguing in Publication Data

Brown, Mara
    Landing on your feet

ISBN 0-07-551377-3

1. Job hunting - Canada. 2. Employees - Canada -
Dismissal of. 3. Job hunting - Canada -
Psychological aspects. 4. Employees - Canada -
Dismissal of - Psychological aspects. I. Title.

HF5382.75.C2B76 1992   650.14'0971   C92-093098-0

This book is sold with the understanding that neither the
author nor the publisher is hereby rendering legal or other
professional advice. If such advice or other assistance is
required, the personal services of competent professional
legal counsel should be sought.

Care has been taken to trace the ownership of any copyright
material contained in this text. The publishers welcome any
information that will enable them to rectify, in subsequent
editions, any incorrect or omitted reference or credit.

Interior Design: Michelle Losier
Cover Design: Dianna Little
Cover Illustration: Shelagh Armstrong
Illustrations: Christopher Griffin

Printed and bound in Canada

To my mother,
whose love, support, and belief
in me allows me to be
all I can be.

ABOUT THE AUTHOR

I was there.

I have always been an achievement-oriented successful person. I graduated in 1983 with an M.B.A. degree from York University with a specialization in Marketing.

I worked in the advertising and promotion industry, climbing up through the ranks, and then was invited to join the "client-side" to run the Marketing and Public Relations department for a major theme park/entertainment attraction. After giving that job "my all" and being a "success" by all indicators, there was a political shake up and I was *jilted*. Just like that.

I've lived through the shock, the anguish, and the grief. I've had my self-esteem battered and shattered. I've learned about friendships and how fragile some of those relationships are. *But I came back.* In fact, I emerged from this awful experience a better person than I was before I got "relocated." (My response upon being told that I was being relocated was, "Oh really, to where?")

Everyone gets kicked in the teeth sooner or later, no matter how good you are, for any number of reasons (for example, politics, budget cutbacks, change in management philosophy, personality conflicts, company buyout). Whatever the reason, there is no shame in getting knocked down. The challenge is in getting up, developing a game plan, and getting on with the rest of your life.

I'd like to help others who have lost their jobs learn how to cope and even prosper from that situation. It is not easy. It takes work, discipline, and perseverance. I did it, and so can others.

I hope that this book helps.

—

CONTENTS

CHAPTER 6 A BLUEPRINT FOR SUCCESS 181

PREFACE

Landing On Your Feet: The Canadian Guide to Surviving, Coping, and Prospering from Job Loss is an almanac of advice. Some things that are written here you may already know. Other information will be new to you. Some parts of this book will remind you of things you may have forgotten, and others may act as a trigger, a jolt, or a source of inspiration.

Take what you can from this book. Refer to it often. It is not meant to be read once and put down. *Landing On Your Feet* should be like a good friend to you. Keep coming back to it for support, practical advice, and guidance. It should become well-worn, like your favourite sweater.

Landing On Your Feet is designed to prod you to think, push you to act, and motivate you to achieve. Some features in this book will be uncomfortable, and perhaps difficult to work through. There are exercises to do that will take time, careful consideration, and deep soul searching. You will only get out of this book what you put into it. Use it to its full potential and you will find yourself able to reach your own full potential.

All periods of growth, transition, and change involve pain. *Landing On Your Feet* will show you ways to deal with your emotions, and will guide you through this difficult time and ease your anguish. You will emerge from this traumatic period of your life a happier and wiser you.

There is so much potential that is still unexplored and untapped in you. This book will take you on a journey of self-discovery and show you options that you may never have known existed, so that you are able to find fulfillment.

The premise of *Landing On Your Feet* is that **being fired was one of the best things that ever happened to you. You have been given an opportunity to learn, grow, and develop yourself and reach levels of happiness and success you never thought possible!**

Landing On Your Feet will make going through job loss easier for you. My hope is that it will also motivate and maybe even inspire you to achieve all that you can achieve and win in the game of life. You deserve it, and you *can* do it! Remember, it is always darkest before dawn, so never give up.

GOOD LUCK!

ACKNOWLEDGEMENTS

I would like to heartily thank the following business leaders of Canada who so generously shared their time, thoughts, and insights with me, so that I could pass on their esteemed philosophies to others. Thank you, David Barbour (Executive Vice President, Labatt Breweries of Canada); Conrad Black (Chairman and C.E.O., Hollinger Inc.); John Cassaday (President and C.E.O., CTV Television Network Ltd.); Hershell Ezrin (Senior Vice President, The Molson Companies, and former Principal Secretary and Deputy Minister to the former Premier of Ontario); Dr. James Gillies (Professor and Founding Dean, The Faculty of Administrative Studies, York University); Paul Godfrey (President and C.O.O., The Toronto Sun Publishing Group, and former Chairman of Metropolitan Toronto); Douglas Grindstaff (President, Procter and Gamble Inc.); Jay Marciano (Senior Vice President, MCA Concerts Canada); Frank Stronach (Chairman, Magna International Inc.); and Moses Znaimer (President and Executive Producer, Citytv and MuchMusic); for your invaluable contributions.

My sincere appreciation to the following lawyers: Larry Banack, Paul Chadwick, Marty Herman, Jeffrey Hoffman, Derek Rogers, and Louis Silverstein, whose advice and legal opinions were so helpful to me.

I would also like to thank the outplacement specialists Sy Eber; Robin Hazel; Sylvia Milne; Ralph Shedletsky; Adria Trowhill; and executive recruiter, Rick Chad; and educational consultant, Cindy Butler; for their important help and guidance.

A special thanks to all those people who have so kindly, graciously, and candidly shared their personal stories with me, so that we all could benefit and learn from their experiences. Their names have been changed (unless a full name is used) to protect their anonymity.

I would like to thank Don Loney and the staff at McGraw-Hill Ryerson Limited for believing in me and in this book. I would also like to thank Greg Howitt, Donald Martin, and Ron Moore, each for their own special support.

And, of course, my wholehearted gratitude to my family, for putting up with me and always being there for me.

~

INTRODUCTION

Downsizing, re-organizing, streamlining, restructering, and relocation are the euphemisms of the nineties. These are all terms to describe the work force reduction that is taking place due to leveraged buyouts, unfriendly takeovers, mergers and acquisitions, new technology and, of course, the economic conditions. Headlines scream at us:

"McDonnell to eliminate 17,000 jobs"
"Pan Am to chop 44,000 jobs"
"G.M. to lay off 15,000 workers"
"DeHavilland may cut 1,800 jobs"
"White collar layoffs looming at Ford"
"Air Canada to lay off 2,900 workers"
"Canadian National Railways plan to reduce management staff by 1,500"
"Auto Big Three to cut white collar work force"

The economic boom of the eighties led to a massive executive overload in the nineties, and corporations are scrambling to re-organize in an effort to become more competitive and trim off any fat that exists in their ranks. Much of the excess is around the middle level of management. Some companies can no longer afford to pay out as many senior level executive salaries as they did in the last decade. Therefore, the hardest hit segment of the newly unemployed is the white collar worker. They are a product of the economy. There are not enough jobs any more to go around. These hard-working, hard-driving, fast-tracking, well-credentialed, success-oriented executives are finding themselves out of work for probably the first time in their lives.

To these people, their career is not just a job; rather, what they do for a living is an integral part of their identity. To be unemployed is a gut-wrenching, devastating, isolating ordeal for these executives who never thought that it could happen to them. The emotional response to job loss is equated with that of divorce or the loss of a loved one. It is a rough, rocky road to travel.

Landing On Your Feet is a road map to guide and help people along their journey to re-employment. This book will be useful to those who fear that their job is in jeopardy, those who have just been terminated, or those who have been grappling with their new-found freedom for a while (or as David Letterman puts it, those who have received a "lifestyle downsizing opportunity"). This book is also for those who feel that their job is safe and secure because it is always good to be prepared and to know what to expect in case being fired is in their future.

Unfortunately, the economic forecast is gloomy, and even when the recession is over, recovery will be slow. In the nineties, businesses will be operating in a world-wide, competitive marketplace, and predictions are that many of the jobs that have been lost will not be replaced. Therefore, this downsizing of the job market is not a short-term trend. Corporations recognize that they must restructure and streamline to more efficiently and effectively compete in the fast-paced global economy of the nineties. Therefore, there will continue to be a littering of white collars in the street as the ranks of middle and senior management become leaner and meaner.

Most executives are starting to realize that old assumptions may not necessarily hold true any more. No longer does getting a good education, working hard, and serving your company loyally ensure that you will be rewarded with a steady progression up the corporate ladder. These managers now recognize that they may have to come face to face with job loss at some point in their career. To many, this unthinkable fate will become all too real.

Job loss is a heartbreaking, painful experience, but the process can be made easier to endure and recover from if you know what to expect and what to do. *Landing On Your Feet* will be full of straightforward advice, memorable quotes, and important information. It will have stories of people who have not only recovered from being fired, but have gone on and achieved great sucess in their careers. My hope is that this book can help, guide, motivate, and maybe even inspire some people who are forced to cope with the loss of their job.

If one of these people is you, sometimes it helps just to know that you are not alone. You are not. This book will help you to survive, cope, and prosper from you job loss, and you will emerge from this experience a better, wiser, and happier person. I promise.

CHAPTER 1...

What Now?

Emotional Impact

What To Expect

So you've been laid off, axed, terminated, pink-slipped, downsized, canned, dumped, excessed, sacked, de-jobbed, outplaced, discharged, de-recruited, outcounselled, relocated, kicked out, de-hired, given your walking papers. In other words . . . you've been fired.

Do you feel rotten, angry, scared, depressed, anxious, worried, lost, sad, embarrassed, kicked in the stomach, inadequate, out of control, hopeless, worried, hurt, worthless? Do you feel an overwhelming sense of despair, shame, loss, panic, envy, emptiness, anguish, pain, agony, fear? Do you feel that your life is out of control, or that you are a terrible person, or a failure, or a fraud, or that you will never work again?

Are you experiencing insomnia, colds, headaches, high blood pressure, stomach problems, restlessness, changes in appetite, decreased ability to concentrate, loss of sexual drive, a tendency to be accident-prone, a feeling of fatigue that won't go away, a lower frustration tolerance, and a slower reaction time?

Well, take a deep breath, and know that you are not alone. These feelings and reactions are very normal and to be expected. They are typical reactions to an important loss, and make no mistake, job loss is traumatic. When you lose your job you may feel that you have lost everything that is important to you. Your job may have provided you with self-fulfillment and social standing. It did provide structure to your days and security to your life.

Society's Role

The society in which we live is very structured and work oriented. In fact, from about the age of four when we enter nursery school, we embark upon a life-long orientation to structure. We go from nursery school to primary school, to high school, to post-secondary education and usually straight into our first job. We are never without a structure in which to live our lives. Finding yourself out of work and therefore without a structure is very stressful and can lead to feeling isolated from society.

Also, in our society people are often defined by what they do for a living. People equate our jobs with our worth. Then, if we buy into and internalize this, work becomes the embodiment of who we are and what our purpose is. It is hard to get away from this limiting belief. In fact, even the great psychologist Erich Fromm said in the early sixties, "Our society measures people's value as human beings in terms of their success or failure at work." This phenomenon is magnified with senior executives, who often are seen as synonymous with the company they work for, and their commitment to their important role in the company is omnipotent. These executives, who loyally served their company (sometimes at the expense of their families) for many years, suddenly find themselves cut off from their lifeline — their meaning and purpose in life. To feel a powerful sense of betrayal in these circumstances is very understandable.

However, remember that you are much more than your job. Don't lose sight of who you are and what wonderful talents and strengths you have. Look at all your accomplishments over the years, and not just in relation to your career. Look at your *life*. This is a great opportunity to explore and develop the full you. Often our careers happen as a matter of chance. A first job out of school leads to the next job and so on. We rarely stop to think about whether we are on the right track. Being fired gives you the opportunity to closely examine what you want to do with the rest of your life.

Everyone needs to feel worthwhile — that we make a difference. This gives us a sense of dignity. Just because you lost your job does not mean you lost yourself or your worth. It is very important to remember that. However, the loss of a job is a very stressful and painful experience. In fact, the process of coping with the loss of a job is very similar to that of coping with the loss of a loved one or being told that you have a terminal illness. The good news is that losing a job is not the end of your life. In fact, the opposite may very well be the case. However, it is important that you be aware that there is a natural process that you will go through to heal this emotional wound.

> *"We are continually faced by great opportunities brilliantly disguised as insoluble problems."*
>
> — ANONYMOUS

Stages Of Recovery

Recovering from your job loss will take you through four stages:

1. Shock/Denial.
2. Anger.
3. Depression.
4. Acceptance/Understanding.

These emotional stages are natural and part of your healing process. Everyone goes through them. It is important not to deny any of these feelings, but to accept them, express them, let go, and then get on with your life! It helps to know what to expect from these stages and how to best handle each stage, so let's go through them one by one.

STAGE ONE: SHOCK/DENIAL

When you first get the news, your defense mechanisms act to try to protect you from the pain and, in so doing, numb your body and emotions to it. Your mind denies the reality. You go into a temporary state of shock. Typical verbal reactions are

"Oh no. Not me!"
"There must be some mistake!"
"It can't be!"
"I'll straighten it all out."
"They can't do this to me!"

Do any of these responses sound familiar? Or perhaps you just felt such a sense of disbelief that you were too numb to say anything. You can expect to be in shock for awhile. The emotional deadness that you feel can be frightening. You may oscillate between belief and disbelief that this has happened to you. Finally you must accept that this is real. It has happened to you. Then you will enter stage two.

STAGE TWO: ANGER

"Resentment is the ultimate never-leaving-home."

— FRITZ PEELS

Rage. Envy. Resentment. Anger, anger, and more anger. You may feel so angry that you think you will explode!

"How could this have happened to me!"

"I'll show them!"

"Those lousy #$*@##!"

It is typical to be envious of anyone else who is still gainfully employed. This could be your ex–co-workers, friends, and even your spouse. "Why did it have to be me? Why wasn't it Bob down the hall? He is far less competent than I am" is not a foreign thought. This is a very difficult stage for your family and friends to endure because your anger can be randomly displaced in all directions as you blame everyone and yourself for this catastrophe. Probably for the first time in your life you feel completely out of control. This just makes you more enraged.

It is very important not to repress this anger. Let it out. Express your rage (in a safe way that doesn't hurt others of course). Here are some suggestions for releasing your anger:

1. Go to a deserted place (drive to an empty parking lot) and *scream your head off!* Yes, scream as loud as you possibly can. Let it all out.

2. Go into your kitchen and get some (not all) of those glasses and/or plates that you've always hated and find someplace safe and *smash* them to smithereens. A vase you despise will also do the trick.

3. Beat up your pillow. Please do not try this on people (no matter how tempting it may seem at the time).

4. Go to a gym and work out *hard.* Racquet ball and squash are especially good for this purpose. Pretend that little black ball is your ex-boss's head (or whoever else suits your purpose). This is very therapeutic.

5. Go for a run. If you are not in good shape then go for a brisk walk. (If you are taking your dog along for the exercise, please make sure not to kick it.)

6. Put on your favourite dance song and play it *loud* (not too loud — you don't want the neighbours to call the police) and *dance, dance, dance* your feet off.

7. Rearrange your furniture or clean your room, your apartment, your house, or your car like it has never been cleaned before. Do it with all your energy. (You've had practice cleaning, as you recently cleaned out your desk.)

8. Take an aerobics class. You will be so confused by the combinations of steps and so out of breath from jumping around that you will have no energy left for being angry.

9. Play your favourite video game or pinball machine with a vengeance. You will be surprised at the scores you will rack up. That will make you feel proud.

10. Write a letter (address it to anyone that you want) and express all of your feelings of rage, anger, and resentment and why everything is that person's fault. Feel free to use as much colourful language as you want. Then *burn it* or *rip it to shreds.*

There, doesn't that feel better?

There are also things to avoid doing:

1. You may want to have a "drunken" night with your friends. That's okay. Do it once if you need to. After

that try to stay away from alcohol and drugs. It only makes things worse.

2. Avoid taking your anger out on your family and friends. This will naturally happen, but try to minimize this as much as possible.
3. Don't torture yourself with "what ifs."
4. Try not to pull your hair out.
5. Do not fling the cat around by the tail.
6. Avoid hitting yourself over the head, both literally and figuratively.
7. Avoid making decisions in anger that you may regret later.
8. Definitely avoid killing someone — including yourself.

Eventually anger and rage will give way to a feeling of great loss. Then you have entered stage three.

STAGE THREE: DEPRESSION

Sadness, hurt, betrayal, despair, devastation, hopelessness, self-depreciation, condemnation, grief, worry, guilt, sorrow, worthlessness, and pain. These emotions will be your temporary companions. You may wonder if you are strong enough to face each day. (You are.) You may fear that you will never work again. (You will.) You may feel like a failure. (You're not.) Financial concerns will add to your depression. You may worry about your ability to meet your mortgage payments, rent, or car payments. Try to not let these thoughts consume you. Things *will* work out. You may feel very lethargic and unmotivated. This is your time to mourn your loss; however, try not to dwell on self-pity. There are things you can do to combat depression. Let's look at some:

1. *Move!* Just get up off your you-know-what and get moving. Do anything — just do something. You'll be surprised at how energy will flow to meet your movement, but first you have to *move!*

2. Take a nice, hot, relaxing bath. Use your favourite bath suds.

3. Go see a funny movie, watch a comedy on TV, rent your favourite hilarious video. Watch "Saturday Night Live" re-runs, Three Stooges or Laurel and Hardy classics. Do anything that makes you laugh. It has been proven that when you laugh, your body releases endorphins which give you a natural high. It is a great feeling.

4. Get a massage. Get a haircut. Do something to pamper yourself.

5. Take in a stray kitten. Play with it. Enjoy it. Love it.

6. Don't isolate yourself. Accept comfort and support from family and friends. Use the telephone. Stay in touch.

7. Cry. Let it out. It's okay. Really.

8. Make a schedule for your days and stick to it. It will give you some sense of structure and control in your otherwise chaotic world.

9. Get involved; do something for others. The best cure for self-pity is to stop dwelling on your troubles by thinking about and doing something else. Volunteer for a cause that you believe in. Giving brings joy.

10. Clean up. Cook a creative meal. The key is (not to belabour the point) to *be active, keep busy!*

Again, stay away from alcohol. It may numb the pain for a short period of time, but alcohol acts as a depressant and therefore the eventual effect will be greater depression. The same holds true for drugs. A momentary "high" and its inevitable "low" will just make things worse. Good nutrition is also important. Try to limit your intake of junk food, sugar, and fatty foods. Most importantly, try to keep from feeling sorry for yourself as much as possible.

If you feel that you've lost everything, that the pain hurts so badly you want to die, then think about this: You can still walk, you can still see, you can still hear, you can still talk, you can still feel (as you are currently so acutely aware), and you still have your loved ones. Now, have you really lost everything? Go for a walk. Take some time and smell the flowers. Notice how beautiful they are. Wake up early and watch the sunrise. Enjoy the sunset in the evening. Listen to the birds. Go to a playground and watch the children play. Take in everything. There is still so much wonder in the world. Focus on what is beautiful to you and what you do have and be grateful for it. So you lost your job. So what. You will get another job — an even better job. You still have you. Life is not over. You are not finished or washed up. Instead, this is your new beginning.

In fact, losing your job can be a blessing in disguise. Were you really happy at your job? Did you feel challenged or were you just coasting? Did you feel appreciated or taken for granted? Did you feel self-fulfilled or bored? Did you look forward to Monday mornings with enthusiasm and excitement, or was your motto "Thank God It's Friday"? Was there someone in the office who just drove you up a wall? Did your boss frustrate you? Looked at in that perspective, was being fired so bad? Even if you did love your job, this can be an opportunity for self-development. Challenge yourself to grow from this. Many very successful people have been fired and they say that being fired was the best thing that happened to them. It pushed them out of a job they probably wouldn't have left and in so doing forced them to re-evaluate their lives and achieve far more success than they otherwise would have. As one great philosopher (my mother) always says, "Things usually happen for the best, although we may not realize it at the time."

Let's look at the story of Mark Breslin. It exemplifies many of the things that we have discussed so far.

➤ "I graduated from university with a degree in English Literature. I really didn't know what I wanted to do. I ended up getting a job at Harbourfront (a Toronto lakefront tourist attraction) programming entertainment. It was my first *real* job and I was really excited about it. Harbourfront was the kind of place that was more than just a job. It became a very important part of my life. I would work six days a week and then on my day off I would go back there to ensure things were running smoothly. It was the most wonderful job I could imagine. During my two years there I worked my way up to be the Director of Theatre and Music (which was the third in command of the programming wing). Things couldn't be better. I was even getting numerous accolades in the press!

"Approximately eighteen months into my tenure, there was a political shake-up. New people were running the show. Six months later when my contract was up for renewal, it was not renegotiated. I was totally shocked. I couldn't believe it! I mean, I was doing such a great job and being publicly recognized for it. I was told to clear out my desk within the week. I was so devastated. To me it wasn't just losing a job, it meant losing my career, for there were very few opportunities in programming at that time. I had also grown so attached to the people I worked with (they were like a surrogate family to me) that I felt lost and totally alone. By the way, my real family was not supportive at that time which made things even harder on me. Their response was, 'I told you so...It's still not too late to go to law school.' My self-esteem was shattered and I was living off unemployment insurance.

"One of the programs I ran at Harbourfront was a comedy night. When I left they abandoned it. I loved running this program and it was very successful. With Harbourfront no longer interested in the program I decided to run it on my own. I put things together quickly, and a few months later I was running weekly comedy shows out of the community centre basement. Yuk Yuks was born. Now I'm so glad that they let me go because had they not done that I would have wound up working for a pittance for the Harbourfront Corporation, and probably never would have started my own business. Now my company is worth twelve million dollars; I have a chain of comedy clubs coast to coast, and I have a subsidiary career as a writer and as a television producer. None of this would have happened if I had not been fired. Of course I couldn't see that at the time. I was too humiliated and devastated. But now, looking back, I guess I have Harbourfront to thank for firing me and therefore making me a successful businessman."

"Whatever the universal nature assigns to any man at any time is for the good of that man at that time."
— Marcus Aurelius

Stage Four: Acceptance/Understanding

You will reach a point after the shock has worn off, after the anger has been vented, and after the sorrow has been expressed, where you accept the situation and it's time to move on with your life. Say goodbye to the old and hello to the new. The mourning of your job loss is over and it is time to move ahead. Let go. The worst is behind you. Now it's time to build a better future!

It's time to "pick yourself up, dust yourself off, and start all over again" (as the old song goes). No one ever said it's going to be easy. It will take courage and determination. There will be setbacks along the way, good days and bad days, ups and downs. But you will find, emerging from all this, a stronger, wiser, happier, and better you. You'll see. It's true.

"Accept the challenges, so that you may feel the exhilaration of victory."
— General George S. Patton

Practical Aspects

"It is one of life's laws that as soon as one door closes, another opens. But the tragedy is that we look at the closed door and disregard the open one."

— André Gide

The Termination Meeting

- Don't sign anything.
- Don't argue — it's pointless.
- Try not to cry. Try to remain calm, cool, and collected.
- Ask what they are prepared to offer. If they have an offer in writing, take it with you. You will be in no shape to objectively evaluate any offer. Tell them you need time to think things over and that you will get back to them.
- Leave with dignity.
- Go to see a lawyer.
- As soon as possible after the termination meeting, make a written note of what was said at that meeting. Because this is usually such an emotional time, you might block out some of what was said at the meeting; however, if you do end up proceeding to litigation, what was said at that time could prove helpful to your case.

To Do And Not To Do

Once you've been fired, there are some practical things that should be done right away, and other things that should not be done at all.

1. See a lawyer right away. Get a legal opinion on the offer (or lack thereof). We will cover legal issues

(including how to find a lawyer) in the next section. For now, suffice it to say that the fee that you may have to pay a lawyer is *well* worth it.

2. There are certain things that you should look for in any severance offer. They are:

    *   *Money* — How much and how will it be paid?

    *   *Insurance coverage* — (life, health, disability, car insurance) — Will your coverage be continued during your severance period? If so, with what arrangement? If not, what are your options?

    *   *Letter of reference* — Make sure that you get that letter immediately. Upon firing staff employers are usually at their weakest point because they may feel guilty, remorseful, or embarrassed. Also, make sure that you and your ex-company agree on the reason that will be given for your departure. (It is a good idea to have someone call for you and check out what they are saying about you, as long as it is done in a professional manner.)

    *   *Outplacement or relocation services* — Many companies will offer this service to outgoing executives to help ease their job search process. There are different types of packages ranging from the use of secretarial services, an area to conduct the job search from, and help in résumé writing and interview tips, to video coaching, and psychological and financial counselling. If you are offered this service, be sure to make full use of that help. It is valuable (and expensive) expertise. Don't be suspicious that because your ex-company is footing the bill, the outplacement or relocation firms are acting as a pipeline back to the company. They are not. Do not turn your back on this assistance. It could prove invaluable. (We will examine outplacement/relocation services further in Chapter 5.)

There are also some extras that could be negotiated:

- continued use of company car,
- continued payment of club dues,
- payment of moving expenses,
- vacation pay, and
- payment of bonuses.

Keep in mind that these payments will only last during your severance period.

3. Look at the tax implications of your severance package. Usually, severance payments are fully taxable as regular income. However, if you are in your late fifties or early sixties, you can handle your termination as early retirement. This will enable you to roll over your pension income into an RRSP, or take some of your severance as a retiring allowance and transfer that into an RRSP. It is important to know your options. Check with a professional on the tax treatment that is best for you. Your lawyer should be able to advise you on this matter.

4. Apply for unemployment insurance. There is no shame in it. You have paid into this fund your entire working life. It is like any other type of insurance. When you need it, you collect. It is that simple. You will have to wait in line to sign up, but, after that, the cheques come by mail. Unemployment insurance payments will not kick in until two weeks after termination or until your severance period of payment is over. Your qualification for benefits and the amount that you can collect depends on your situation. The period of time that you are eligible to get payments will vary by the level of unemployment in the area in which you live. Be sure to check with your local unemployment insurance office so that you will know what your entitlement is.

5. Make sure you have an answering machine or an answering service. If you need to buy one (you can

get a good machine for under $100), get one that
enables you to call in for messages. Have your outgo-
ing message in your voice and make it professional.
As cute as those funny little messages are, they are
not appropriate at this time. Also, every time you
answer the telephone, act as if it is a prospective
employer on the other end. This could save some of
those little embarrassing moments. If you do not live
alone, you may want to have another line or call-
waiting installed. This could ease a lot of tension in
your household (especially if you have teenagers)
and will not cost a lot of money.

6. Get your own personal "business" card. To get the
   card made, go to a local copy or print shop. They will
   have different paper stocks, font styles (for example
   this is one font style; whereas this is another;
   and this is yet another; and this yet another; do you get
   the idea?), and inks to choose from. They will also
   have many different examples of cards that you can
   look at. Choose what you like or design your own,
   and the shop should be able to have several hundred
   cards ready for you within one week. Depending on
   paper stock and ink selection, the cost for a couple
   hundred cards (and you will want to order no less
   than 250 to 500 cards) will be anywhere from approximately $150 and up. The least expensive route
   is to pick a regular white stock with a black ink. It is a
   good idea to go to several copy or print shops and
   get quotes, as prices may vary from store to store.
   The card should have your name, address, and
   phone number on it. Additional information that you
   may want to include could be educational degrees
   (for example, M.B.A., C.A., L.L.B., etc.) or business
   specialties (for example, Marketing Specialist, Financial Analyst, Business Consultant, etc.). Use these
   cards as you would have used your business card in
   the past. Be sure to give your card to anyone you
   meet who could be in a position to help you. Having

the card will add to your professionalism as you will
not be fumbling for a pen and paper at inopportune
moments.

7. Put together a budget. If you are married, do this
budgeting process together with your spouse. Add
up all your necessary expenses (rent, mortgage, car
payments, utilities, phone, food, etc.) and all your
sources of income (severance money, unemployment
insurance following the severance period, interest on
investments, income from your spouse, etc.). From
this, figure out a monthly budget and stick to it. You
may have received financial counselling as part of
your outplacement package. Go see that counsellor
immediately and, if you are married, bring your
spouse with you. Knowing your financial position will
alleviate some of the stress of wondering where you
stand.

8. Network. Network. Network. Call anyone and everyone you know who could even remotely be in a
position to help you. Tell them your situation. Don't
be ashamed, embarrassed, or afraid to ask for help.
Even the Bible says "Ask and you shall receive." You
will be surprised at how many people know someone
who knows someone who can help you. If you don't
ask, you won't get. Asking for help when you need it
can open many doors for you. You will find that most
people will be happy to assist you. Accept their help
with appreciation. One day you will be able to assist
another. It is also a good idea to maintain your mem-
bership in (or join) industry associations. This will
help you keep in touch with issues and people. (We
will examine networking further in Chapter 5.)

9. Join a self-help or support group. There are groups
such as E.A.R.N. in Toronto and Forty Plus in the
United States that were started by executives who
were fired to help other fired executives. If there
is currently not such a group in your city, then start

one. It can be as simple as putting an advertisement in your local newspaper asking recently fired executives to contact you. In support groups, you will be surrounded by those who are facing similar situations as yourself and the practical and emotional help gleaned from groups such as these is invaluable. In fact, you may want to find someone in the group and use the "buddy system" that groups such as Alcoholics Anonymous have found so helpful. This kind of emotional support is very important and can make a big difference in your ability to cope with this very difficult time.

Let's look at the story of Colleen Clarke, the founder of the support group The Executive Advancement Resource Network (E.A.R.N.) in Toronto.

"I had worked in shopping centre management for many years when I decided to make a career change. I went to work for a retail leasing company. Nine months later they had to close down a development department (due to economic conditions) and let twenty people go. I was out the door. I was unemployed. I did some soul searching and tried to figure out what I wanted to do with my life. I decided that I would like to get into the field of training and development, and tried to learn about the industry and networked until all my networking sources had dried up. I found no job openings in that field. I felt in limbo, and totally misdirected and confused. I didn't know what to do. There were no shopping centre management or leasing jobs available; in fact, I couldn't even get an interview in either of those fields. I was at a dead end. I had no direction and no focus. It was my lowest point.

"I had a lot of empty time and no one to share it with. I realized that I had to do something to generate some new activity in my life. I thought that there must be other people out there in the same boat as me, and wouldn't it be great if we could find each other, get together and share information, contacts, social time, and emotional support. I decided to place a small classified ad in the local newspaper: "Unemployed professional? If you are looking to share some networking skills, recreation time, and emotional support call this number. . ." After the ad ran, two people called. It was a start.

"I then found out that there was a group similar to the one I wanted to form that started in New York City. That made me realize that the idea was feasible. Based on my belief that there was a need for this type of group, I called the media myself and explained what I wanted to do. The media was very supportive and the following week two articles appeared in the papers. Those articles generated *ninety* phone calls! (Talk about the power of the media!) The calls went through the Self-Help Clearing Centre of Toronto. That weekend I telephoned every person back on that list and arranged for us all to meet on the following Friday.

"Then I sat down and thought about what to do at this meeting. 'What do I want from this? What would other people want to know?' These were questions that I asked myself. I set up an agenda for that first meeting and hoped that I was on the right track. I had no idea what I was doing. And I was still feeling really low and very down on myself, but at least now I was busy during the day and I had a purpose. That helped. Then I asked people at the meeting what it was they wanted from these meetings. A few of us sat down and set out some specific goals for the group. We wanted this group to give emotional support, find hidden job leads, and teach practical and helpful job search skills. A certain amount of emotional support comes from having new friends with things in common. You know they understand how you. Even just to have your phone ring more often helps you to feel less isolated.

"To be honest, I was totally surprised by the incredible response to the group, and did not think I was really prepared to handle it. However, it seemed like I had a sort of guiding force helping me along the way. Things just seemed to naturally and easily fall into place. All of a sudden there was energy, synergy, and a feeling of rapport in the group. It started to take on a life of its own! It is very much like a team. The success of this group lies in the nature of the group itself. People give so much of themselves and their time. Members telephone each other, get together for coffee, have each other over for dinner, and are genuinely caring and supportive.

"I am continually surprised to see how people lower their barriers and open up their hearts and their feelings to each other in this group. We share the anguish and the joy. (Each week usually one member of our group gets a job.) Members feel comfortable and are able to let out their feelings in a genuinely supportive, caring, and understanding environment. Guest speakers who come to talk to the group invariably tell me that it meant a great deal to them to speak to our group because they were able to help so many people who were really grateful for the advice.

"There are a lot of people out there who are happy to help. It is just a matter of asking for that help. That was one of the biggest problems I had to overcome — the fear of asking. I used to even have difficulty asking my roommate to feed my cat if I was away for a day! So, for the first month of the group's existence I did everything myself because I couldn't bring myself to ask for help. Then it became overwhelming and I had to confront my fear. I did. It is incredible how easy it is to get help when all you have to do is ask! Now I feel that the group does everything. Everyone is so generous.

"The thing that touches me the most, though, is the impact this group seems to have on its members. For example, one member told me: 'My wife has seen such an incredible change in me since I've started coming to E.A.R.N. This group has made me a much happier person, and as a result of that, our relationship is better; so anything that this group offers, I do. I come home a happier guy and therefore my whole family life is happier.' Another person in our group was going through a terrible time, with a wrongful dismissal action and a new baby to deal with. He was really experiencing a loss of self-worth. When he first started coming to E.A.R.N., he reminded me of a dog walking around with its tail between its legs. It was heart-breaking. The group members telephoned him regularly, and got together with him often for lunch or coffee. After he was in the group for about one month the change in him was incredible. He now helps other members with their résumés, and has them over to his place for dinner and participates in the group as a volunteer leader. He is a changed person! He tells me that he is so thankful for what the group has given him that he tries to give back two- to three-fold to the group.

"E.A.R.N. gave him a sense of belonging and a feeling of usefulness and purpose again. It seems that this group has had an impact on so many people's ability to cope and move forward with their lives. I am very happy for them. Everyone does it themselves with a little help from a group of people that care. I do not take the credit."

—

By the way, Colleen Clarke is now employed at an outplacement firm. She got the job through networking with the people in the group. Her job is not only in the field she wanted to break into (training and development), but she now runs E.A.R.N. as a part of her job. She did not just get a job; she is doing what she loves. The 350 members of E.A.R.N. would say she deserves all the good things in the world that come her way. She has helped so many and given so many others a forum in which to help themselves.

> *"It is one of the most beautiful compensations of this life that no man can sincerely try to help another without helping himself."*
> — RALPH WALDO EMERSON

10. Put together or update your résumé. It will be your major job search tool. The importance of a good

résumé cannot be stressed enough. Outplacement and relocation services provide assistance with résumé writing. We will cover the topic of résumés in Chapter 5.

11. Something mentioned earlier bears repeating: do volunteer work for a cause you believe in. This will not only get you out of the house and keep you busy (which will help alleviate self-engrossed self-pity), but it will broaden your horizons and could even lead to a job. Either way, you will feel useful and productive and that will help you to put back the pieces of your shattered self-image. Doing something worthwhile will make you feel good. Helping those less fortunate will also help you to put your own problems in perspective.

12. Make a schedule for your days and stick to it. Get out of the house and away from your bed, television, and refrigerator. The worst thing that you can do is continually oversleep and mope around the house. If you did not get outplacement facilities from which to conduct your job search, then set aside a part of your house or apartment as your work area. Use this area specifically for your job search work. Make sure your work area has a phone, paper, pens, and files in it. This is your new office. Also, because the job of looking for a job is so stressful, schedule some pampering, relaxation, and enjoyable parts to your day. Try to exercise regularly as part of your daily routine and eat right to keep your body strong to help ward off the negative physical effects of stress.

13. Get a library card. It is free. Read books on subjects that interest you. Read funny books. Read motivational books or lose yourself in an exciting fantasy book. Research companies that interest you. A library card is a wonderful thing to have. (And what a bargain!) It can open up exciting worlds for you.

14. Try not to dwell on the negative; try to see things on the positive side. Think good thoughts! (More on this later.)

"All things are difficult before they are easy."
— John Norley

Legal Issues
The Law

The law is a very precarious subject. There are often many different ways to apply the rules, and outcomes can rarely be assured. The law is not black and white; it displays itself in many shades of grey.

In Canada, an employer can terminate an employee for any reason, or even without a reason at any time. There are two exceptions to this:

1. If the termination was based on discriminatory grounds, then the employee's rights are governed by the Human Rights Code. One's recourse through the Human Rights Commission can allow for damages and reinstatement.

2. If the termination was a unionized situation, then the Labour Relations Act applies. Almost without exception, a person who belongs to a trade union and who has entered into a collective agreement will find recourse within the collective agreement. There is usually no independent right to sue in this case because the employment contract is not entered into between the individual employee and the company, instead there is the bargaining agent who acts as the intermediary.

Each of these federal statutes has, within it, its own process for recourse and reinstatement.

This book is not a comprehensive or exhaustive examination of labour law. It will not provide you with definitive legal answers. Instead, it will focus on terminations that are not governed by the above two statutes, and will attempt to give you an overview of pertinent legal issues.

Just Cause

While an employer can fire an employee at will, if the termination is without "just cause" (which is a judicially defined term), then the employee is legally entitled to reasonable notice of termination or payment in lieu of that notice. If the employee does not receive this notice, then legal recourse is available through either government intervention, as dictated through the employment statutes, or through the courts to sue for all the income that would have otherwise been received during that period of reasonable notice.

If an employer can prove that the employee was fired for "just cause" and the employer has proper documentation of this, then the terminated employee is not entitled to any notice, and therefore is entitled to receive *nothing*. There are general rules which define conduct (or shall we say misconduct) that can justify dismissal for "just cause." However, each case is reviewed individually based on its own facts. The behaviours that the courts usually recognize as sufficient cause for dismissal without notice are:

- fraudulent misrepresentation of credentials,
- conflict of interest,
- gross insubordination/willful disobedience/insolence,
- substance abuse or intoxication on company premises,
- activities that seriously endanger fellow employees or the employer's property,
- breach of trust,
- theft, fraud, or any dishonest or criminal activity,
- chronic absenteeism or lateness,
- illness,
- or any other misconduct that the court deems serious.

If your employer has terminated you for "just cause," and you don't agree, be sure to get professional legal advice.

When you go to see your lawyer, have all your documentation against the company's accusations prepared (memos,
letters, etc.) and bring it with you. Being organized when
visiting your lawyer will save you time and money.

If, however, you were let go with no "just cause," then
you are entitled to receive reasonable notice of that termination or payment in lieu of that notice. The key question
then becomes one of reasonable notice.

What Is Reasonable Notice?

There are two areas of law that answer this question:

1. The provincial statutes by which the legislatures or
    parliaments have established minimum standards of
    entitlement and procedures. Each province has its
    own statute. For the purpose of this book, the Em-
    ployment Standards Act (which is Ontario's statute)
    will be used as the example of provincial legislation.
    In fact, most provincial acts are similar to that of
    Ontario (except for Quebec).

2. Common law is like a cloud that floats above the
    minimum provincial requirements. Common law
    cannot reduce the legislative standards; it serves to
    increase those standards.

It is important to note that neither provincial employment
statutes nor common law allow for re-instatement of position. A suit for wrongful dismissal is not about the loss of
your job (as we said earlier, the employer can terminate
any position at will; their only obligation is to give proper
notice); rather, it is about the fairness of the length of notice (or payment in lieu of that notice) offered. It is an action to compensate you for the actual loss incurred, *not* to
right a wrong. For example, if you lost an arm, you may be
able to sue for damages, but no matter how good your lawyer is, or how much money you are awarded, nothing can
give you back your arm. It is the same with your job. Keep
that in mind.

Getting back to that all important question of reasonable notice, the provincial employment standards legislation dictates notice periods that are based solely on length of service. For example, the Employment Standards Act of Ontario provides required notice periods as follows:

Period of Employment	Notice Period
more than or equal to 3 months; but less than 1 year	1 week
more than or equal to 1 year; but less than 3 years	2 weeks
more than or equal to 3 years; but less than 4 years	3 weeks
more than or equal to 4 years; but less than 5 years	4 weeks
more than or equal to 5 years; but less than 6 years	5 weeks
more than or equal to 6 years; but less than 7 years	6 weeks
more than or equal to 7 years; but less than 8 years	7 weeks
more than or equal to 8 years	8 weeks

Also, if the employer's annual payroll exceeds $2.5 million, then notice can increase to a maximum of 20 weeks.

These notice periods are minimum standards. (Keep in mind that other factors may also apply, this is a simplification.) However, in the case of executive termination, these minimum standards are usually perceived to be inadequate. That is when common law will apply. Unless there is a specific employment contract, the courts assume that the employment term is of indefinite duration. If there is an employment contract that explicitly outlines the term of employment or defines what constitutes reasonable notice (as long as it over and above the provincial statutory minimum period), then that may be binding. However, if the court finds that the notice period as stated in the contract is insufficient, the contract will probably not be enforced. If an employment contract is for a specific job or time period, and the employee is kept on even one day past that contractual agreement, without any mention of the termination of the contract, then the courts could look at that as an indefinite period of employment, and common law would then be applicable. If an employment contract is over and is not renewed, there is usually no legal recourse.

Under common law, there is no set of rules or laws for determining what constitutes reasonable notice upon firing. Each case is judged individually based on its own facts. However, there are certain variables that the courts will consider. These are:

a) Length of employment at the company.

b) The age of the employee (the courts will assume that the older the employee is, the more difficult it will be to find comparable employment; therefore, the length of notice may increase).

c) The position of the employee in the company (the nature and character of employment).

d) Whether the employee was enticed away from another company (induced to leave secure employment to join the company). If that is the case, the notice period may be increased.

e) The economic position of the company.

f) Availability of similar employment.

It is interesting to note that courts will acknowledge recessionary pressures on both the discharged employee and the discharging company. Here are two widely quoted legal decisions that were made during the recession of the early eighties that take differing positions on the issue of reasonable notice.

Bohemier v. Storwall International (1982)

"... An employee may be dismissed either on reasonable notice or by payment in lieu of notice. The latter alternative is almost invariably selected because, for obvious reasons, it is not helpful to a business to continue to employ a person who has received notice of dismissal. Payment in lieu of notice involves a cost to the employer for which there is no corresponding production or benefit. In my view, there is a need to preserve the ability of an employer to function in an unfavorable economic climate. He must, if he finds it necessary, be able to reduce his work force at a reasonable cost. If he cannot do so, the alternative may be bankruptcy or receivership. It seems to me that when employment is unavailable due to general economic conditions, there has to be some limit on the period of notice to be given to discharged employees even if they are unable to secure similar employment within the notice period."

Misovic v. Acres Davey McKee Ltd. (1983)

". . . If I correctly apprehend the present state of our law, reasonable notice must be given in circumstances where there is no cause for termination; the purpose of notice is to afford an employee a reasonable period of time to obtain similar employment. If this is so, then to award an employee substantially less damages (in lieu of reduced notice) in adverse economic conditions (when similar employment is obviously more difficult and, in this case, was not available), negates the basic principle of the employee's entitlement to reasonable notice."

As these decisions illustrate, there are great differences in the application of principals in determining what constitutes reasonable notice.

The Duty To Mitigate Damages

Under common law, there is a duty for you to mitigate your damages. That means that you must make every effort to find suitable alternative employment. If you do not make this effort and your former employer can show that to be true, you will receive far less in compensation from the courts. If you are considering starting your own business instead of looking for alternate employment, take note. If you are readily employable (good work history, good credentials, reasonably young, and are in an occupation for which there is demand),

and you ignore any job search possibilities and launch immediately into a new business, with the expectation that it will lose money initially, and you get involved in litigation, you may face the allegation that you have not done your best to mitigate your damages. However, if you can demonstrate to the court that there was a lack of opportunity in your field of expertise and that this was the most viable option, then you can justify starting your own business.

Damages

Wrongful dismissal cases are based on the legal premise of breach of contract. An implied indefinite contract is assumed when you are employed (unless there is a contract that states otherwise). If, when fired, you are not given the requisite notice, than that is legally viewed as a breach of contract and hence you are entitled to collect damages arising from that breach. Your entitlement of damages is largely based upon what happens to you (what loss you actually suffer) after termination. For example, if a dismissed employee finds alternate comparable work for the same salary and benefits right away, then that employee has not suffered a loss and is therefore not entitled to any damages. This is an important concept to keep in mind when assessing whether or not to litigate.

It is currently estimated that in this economy, it will take a senior-level executive approximately eight months to a year to find comparable re-employment. Therefore, if you are a senior executive and have been offered a severance package for eight months, realize that that is a borderline offer. Also keep in mind that if you are offered a package for let's say, six months, and your legal entitlement is estimated at the ten- to twelve-month range, if you sue, in order to collect the ten months' wages, you must have been unemployed for those ten months, or employed at a lesser income than you would have earned at your old job. It is often a question of judgement in terms of how realistic the offer is relative to everyday practical issues, such as, the length of time you think that it will take to find re-employment. In the above example, if that dismissed employee thinks that it will take less than six months to find a job, then the severance offer of six months should be accepted.

The severance package that you are offered must be balanced against all these issues, plus, keep in mind that there is usually a greater financial and emotional need for the severance money right after termination as opposed to later when you will most likely be re-employed.

How To Find A Lawyer

1. The best way to find a lawyer is through personal referral.

   a) Ask people you know, or your family lawyer if they know a good labour relations or employment lawyer that they can refer you to. (Only ask people whose judgement you trust.)

   b) The company that you worked for has a law firm that acts on its behalf. That firm can't represent you, but it will be able to recommend a good lawyer for you whose opinion they respect. (By the way, this could help in the negotiation process.)

   c) If you have been given outplacement or relocation services as part of your severance package, ask them to recommend a good lawyer for you. These firms are well tuned into the employment and labour legal community.

2. If however, for some reason you don't know anyone who can refer you to a good labour relations lawyer, each province has its own Law Society and it will assist you. For example, in Ontario, the Law Society of Upper Canada offers a Lawyer Referral Service. (The phone number is (416) 947-3330.) Tell them that you are interested in speaking to a Labour Relations lawyer, and they will give you a few names (usually three) of lawyers in your geographic area that you

can call. You are then entitled to a half-hour free consultation. (Not all provinces can offer this free service. Check with the Law Society in your province.) This consultation can be done in person or over the phone. A note of caution: this is a voluntary system, whereby participating lawyers will have offered their services to the Law Society of Upper Canada. There is no monitoring system set up. Therefore, it is a hit-and-miss approach to finding a lawyer. It is a good idea to talk to more than one lawyer (and since the first half-hour is free, it won't cost you anything to shop around).

If you do not go through the Law Society's Lawyer Referral Service, do not assume that the first half-hour is free. Many lawyers do charge for the first visit. The question of fees should be raised up front.

- Will the lawyer charge for the first meeting?
- What is the lawyer's hourly fee?

You can expect to pay anywhere from $100 to $350 an hour. If you want to hire a big-name lawyer, be aware that they are very expensive. At this point, you may want to watch your money. There are other lawyers available who are just as competent, but because they have a lower profile, they will be less expensive. Whatever the fee, it will be money well spent. Some ex-employers will agree to pay for your legal advice. You may want to check that out.

You And Your Lawyer

During the first meeting (which should be anywhere from half an hour to an hour), briefly describe your situation (job level/title, salary package, circumstances), what offer you have or don't have (if you have a written offer bring it with you), your background, your credentials, and what you think the level of opportunity for re-employment is in your field of expertise. Ask what you are entitled to, then *listen*. And I mean really listen with an open mind. Unfortunately, many people have misconceptions about what their entitlement is, and they allow that to formulate their views before they even walk into a lawyer's office. What they end up doing is looking for a lawyer who will agree with their preconceived notions. Wrong. What you need from a lawyer is realistic, objective advice.

After this initial conversation, an experienced lawyer should be able to assess your situation and evaluate whether the offer you have (or do not have) is reasonable or unreasonable, and what you can legitimately expect in a negotiated settlement or in court. (By the way, unlike cases in which "just cause" is involved, it is not necessary to bring documentation showing your capabilities. In this case, ability is not the legal issue. Having to plow through these materials will only waste the lawyer's expensive time.)

If the second lawyer you speak to tells you something totally different than the first lawyer you spoke to, go see a third. Most good lawyers when given the above information should give you advice that is in the same ballpark in terms of your entitlement. Make sure your lawyer is well versed in recent judicial trends, severance alternatives, and the tax treatment options of severance money. You want to make sure that your lawyer is skilled, practical and balanced (knows the company side and the employee side of the issues and can realistically assess situations), and will take into consideration the personalities involved and truly has your best interest at heart. Use your instincts to guide you in your choice of the best lawyer for you. Not every lawyer is well suited to every client. Remember, you have to feel comfortable with this lawyer, as this is an emotionally charged situation. The client-lawyer relationship is a very personal one. You want to be able to relate to the lawyer you choose to represent you.

Securing legal counsel as early on in the game as possible is a good idea. Your lawyer will advise you as to what to expect and what to do, and will protect your legal position and help you to avoid making costly errors. Frequently the fear of unemployment and the resultant lack of money flowing in can lead newly terminated employees to sign agreements that are not in their best interest. Don't let fear motivate you. Remember what we said earlier in this book: *Make sure that you have good legal advice before you sign anything.* Often companies take negotiations with ex-employees more seriously if they know that the employee is operating under advisement from a lawyer. You may want to be the one to negotiate the severance package with your lawyer acting as your backroom coach behind the scenes carefully stage-directing the process. Or alternatively, you may want to have nothing to do with the negotiation process, and have your lawyer represent you in all dealings with your ex-company. Neither way is right or wrong. Do whatever feels most comfortable to you.

If both you and your lawyer feel that the severance package being offered to you is insufficient or unfair, and all efforts to negotiate a better settlement have been exhausted, you will be faced with the decision of whether or not to litigate.

To Sue Or Not To Sue

That is the gut-wrenching question. Litigation of this nature should never be entered into lightly, and you and your lawyer should carefully examine all variables (and your motivation) before any decision is made.

Litigation can be personally and financially devastating. As the legal process escalates, so do the legal fees. Make sure that you have the financial resources to launch such a costly undertaking. The time involved for these cases to come to trial is also quite lengthy. It often takes up to two years for a case to come to trial, and there is no certainty as to the outcome. Aside from the significant expense of litigation, and the considerable lengthiness of the process, and the uncertainty of the outcome, by far the most destructive part of litigation is the impact it has on your emotions. Psychologically, litigation tends to fixate you in the past at a time in your life when you need to put the past behind you and move on with your life. It keeps you focused on the pain, the hurt, and the betrayal.

The ongoing financial and emotional tension of pursuing litigation can put great additional stress on you and your family. Your spouse should attend all the meetings with your lawyer. In this way, your partner will understand all the issues and options involved (there will not be the problem of miscommunicating or defending the legal advice) and, most importantly, the decision of which path to follow will be a joint decision, one you will both agree to live with.

Another factor to consider is the extent to which a potential employer may be sensitive to the fact that you are suing your former employer. This is even more pronounced in industries where there are few employers, and the more senior your level is in a company. There is less of a stigma attached to being involved in litigation with your former employer; however, although you may no longer be out-and-out blackballed for it, you would be well advised to consider that this may impact on your ability to find appropriate re-employment.

Keep in mind as well, that you may go through the considerable expense of legal action, take it to trial and *win,* and still not be able to collect any money because the company may have gone bankrupt! Unfortunately, in this economy that is a very distinct possibility.

Look Before You Leap

Take all these variables into account and remember, your lawyer can't tell you what to do; rather, he or she can only recommend or advise you. It is always your decision as to what course of action you will take. (A point made earlier that bears repeating is that a wrongful dismissal action is not about the dismissal. Rather, it is about the notice period or payment in lieu of notice. The courts will assess what you would have earned during that period and that is what they can award you. It is a case about money. You cannot be reinstated in your old job.)

Very few companies today get frightened by the threat of a lawsuit; however, it is in the employer's best interest to wrap this issue up as neatly and as quickly as possible. It is very distracting and destructive to have a lawsuit pending. Therefore, if the company makes you a severance offer, don't feel pressured to accept it right away. Even if the offer is made with an expiry date of acceptance, the offer may still be valid after that date has passed. There is nothing wrong with waiting, or with trying to improve the offer. However, be sure not to close any doors by saying such door-slamming statements as "Do it my way or I'll sue you!" or, "I will not accept that under any circumstances!"

Litigation

Perhaps your former company acted in a deceitful or reprehensible way. Perhaps they are offering you next to nothing for a severance payment. Whatever your reasons (and I hope that the reason is not based on revenge), if you decide to litigate be prepared for a long, tough battle. Here are some tips that could help you through:

1. Keep a detailed record of *everything* you do in your efforts to find a job (phone calls, letters, networking, lunches, discussions, etc.) on a daily basis. Also keep track of all your expenses relating to your job search (stamps, paper, printing, gas, parking, mileage, meals, etc.) because all reasonable expenses relating to your effort to mitigate your damages (find a job) could be compensated for. Being organized and prepared can make all the difference in the success or failure of your case.

2. Keep a diary of your emotional feelings. Not only will it be a good release, but it may be used for evidence. See your doctor if you are not feeling well physically or emotionally and make sure your doctor takes note of your symptoms. Keep all your bills for prescriptions and out-of-pocket doctor expenses.

3. Have a professional call your former employer and find out what is being said about you. If it is positive, it can help your case later on; if it is unjustly negative ... well, there are laws that protect against defamation of character. It will also be useful in your job search to know what potential employers will hear when they do a reference check.

4. Always act with integrity. Do not speak badly of your former company and certainly do not inflict any damage to any of its property.

5. Be strong and hang in there.

> *"You are part of the universe, no less than the stars and the trees, and you have a right to be here. Whether it is clear to you or not, no doubt the universe is unfolding as it should."*
>
> — DESIDERATA

CHAPTER 2...

What Do I Say?

All In The Family

Losing your job is shocking. And devastating. And then you have to go home to your family. What do you say? How do you explain? If you are the breadwinner in your family, you may feel that you have let your family down, and they will think of you as a failure and won't respect you. How will you tell them? Panic may set in. You may find your thoughts drifting to how this would never have happened in "Leave It to Beaver." Ward would never have to come home and tell June, Wally, and the Beav that he was fired! You may play with the idea of not even telling your family at all.

Well, stop and take a deep breath. Again. (By the way, deep breathing is very relaxing and very healthy.) Recognize the fact that losing your job *will* affect your family. It will test its strength and structure. It is like a building losing one of its main support beams. It tests the overall stability of the whole. Because you will be less able to support your family emotionally and, perhaps, financially, others will have to pick up the slack and fill the void that has been made. This will naturally cause tension and pressure. This jolt could throw your family into a crisis situation. Family dynamics and old patterns of behaviour will probably change. There will be a great deal of stress to work through. However, this situation can make your family closer and stronger if handled properly.

Your spouse (or significant other) will be greatly affected by your job loss. He or she will feel the shock and the resentment, will share your fears, your doubts and your feeling of betrayal. Your spouse may panic at the fear of losing security, stability, and social standing, and may feel very confused. He or she will most likely want to be loving, caring, and supportive, but may be feeling emotions that are in conflict with this. For example, your significant other may feel angry at the company for disrupting your lives. Your spouse may also feel anger and resentment towards you. Thoughts like "How could you let this happen" are not uncommon. If your partner feels anger toward you, he or she will undoubtedly feel guilty and embarrassed over feeling that anger and may try to shut it out. It is really important that you realize that although the firing happened to you, your partner is just as much the victim, and will be experiencing all sorts of conflicting, complex and confusing emotions. This initial confusion can lead to increased tension between partners and add pressure to an already stressful situation. It is important to talk about your feelings openly and honestly with each other and remember that these pressures are directly related to your job loss and will ease off when the situation changes.

Your spouse may feel injured, threatened, and scared, and will need reassurance and support. If you are given outplacement services, bring your spouse to some of the meetings. Don't let your partner feel isolated. Involve him or her as much as you can. As you embark upon your job search, make sure that your spouse is aware of what that process entails. Keep your partner updated on your search and as much a part of it as possible. You both must talk honestly with each other and share your concerns. Cry together, plan together, and be strong for each other. Some outplacement firms offer stress-management workshops and group counselling sessions for the spouse and family of the person who got fired to help the family understand the process, the emotions, and the dynamics of job loss. If your family understands your situation fully, they can support you in a more productive manner. You may also want to look for support from someone else who is very close to you, such as a friend, parent, or sibling. It is a good idea to spread your support system around so that you are not relying too heavily on one person.

Unfortunately, some spouses will react with hostility, anger, and harsh resentment. Some marriages will break up. However, there usually would have been a problem with the relationship prior to the job loss, and that added stress was just the proverbial straw that broke the camel's back. If, on the other hand, the marriage is strong and both partners love and respect each other, this trauma can make the relationship even stronger and bring the family closer together. There will be more time to communicate and work together toward a common goal (your re-employment).

Even if you knew that you were going to lose your job (you may have even consulted with a lawyer or a financial consultant in preparation for the event), it is still an emotional shock when it actually happens. When that message is delivered and the inevitable has happened, the emotional impact can never be underplayed. If the job loss comes as a complete surprise, the emotional reaction is magnified. After you've been told of your termination, you may need some time alone (or with an outplacement counsellor) before you go home. Take that time, because how you go home and tell your family the news can have a substantial impact on how your family will mobilize together to support you. If you go home reeling from the shock and are incoherent, or express the incredible anger you feel, your family may feel frightened, hurt, and insecure. If you go home and rant and rave, yelling things such as:

"I'll get them!"
"I'll sue those bastards!"
"They'll be sorry that they ever did this to me!"

your family will not know how to react. They will be scared and it will aggravate an already foreign and stressful situation. So make sure that you calm down as much as possible before you go home and talk to your partner. However, don't put it off for more than a few hours. It is important to tell your spouse as soon as possible, and when you do don't magnify the situation, and don't paint the canvas black. Make an effort to explain what happened and what the company is prepared to do for you. For example, outline the severance package, outplacement services, reference letter, and any other offer the company made to you. Try to present the situation in a reasonable, objective, and positive way. Instead of going home and saying:

"I lost my job today. I'm a failure. I'm so sorry that I've let you down. I don't know what we'll live on or if I will ever find a job again. We're doomed!"

try:

"I lost my job today. It was a shock to me but I was told that it was not due to my job performance. The company offered me a severance package of X months' salary and the services of an outplacement company. They will help me get myself together and be successful in my job search. I feel really lousy now, and I'll need your support and understanding, but I know that we'll be okay."

You are saying the same thing, but the first example described the situation in an alarmist and unrealistically negative manner; whereas the second example was a more calm, objective, and positive way of relaying the situation. This will leave the door to communication open. The first way will slam it shut. The most important thing is to be honest with your family. Share your feelings with your partner. You will both have insecurities, fears, doubts, anger, and hostility to work through. Work through it together.

The worst thing you could possibly do is not tell your family what happened. You may think that by doing this you are protecting them. You couldn't be more wrong. First of all, there may be financial issues that would increase the pressure if you didn't tell your family. Instead you can deflate some financial pressure by discussing major expenditures with your partner. Some expenditures may have to be cancelled, and others (such as vacations) could be postponed. If your family knows about the loss of your job, they can contribute by tightening their belts. If they don't know, they will go on spending as usual. That will add to your stress. Secondly, your family can be an incredible source of support and help to you. If you don't tell them about your termination, then you won't have that support system in place and you will not have that team effort in terms of your job search.

Most importantly, if you don't tell your family about your job loss, and they find out later (which they usually will), your family may feel a huge sense of betrayal and a real disappointment in you. They may wonder why you didn't have faith in them or trust them enough to share this news with them. They may think that you didn't feel they would be supportive enough, or you didn't feel close enough to them, or that they were not important enough to you for you to share such an important event. Keeping this news from them can destroy the bond within a family and make your family feel isolated from you. Not telling your family that you lost your job is risky business. It does not make anything better, and will usually do far more harm than good.

Job loss is incredibly stressful, and when you are under that kind of stress, it comes out in all different kinds of ways. The stress will filter down through your family and everyone will know something is wrong, but they will be powerless to help you if they don't know what it is. That will lead to feelings of frustration and potential conflict.

Let's learn from the story of Eric W:

"When I was fired it came as a complete shock to me. I truly couldn't believe it. I was told on a Tuesday afternoon. I felt like an incredible failure. I mean, my role in the family was to bring home the bacon. I felt that I could no longer do what any good husband should do . . . support my family. I left the office and wandered the streets. I went to a park and sat on a bench and felt like a bum. I kept asking myself, 'How could I tell my family?' My wife and I just had a baby girl eight months earlier, and we had a four-year-old son and a seven-year-old daughter. How could I tell my kids that their daddy was all washed up? My family needed to be supported. The kids needed new clothes all the time (they grow so fast) and then there were the mortgage payments, the car payments, and on and on. I felt overwhelmed!

"I was offered a severance package of six months' salary. If we were careful, we could probably cover ourselves for eight months. I didn't think about that at the time. I was too busy panicking. I decided to 'protect' my family and not worry them. In reality, I just couldn't bring myself to tell them. I was too embarrassed. I was sure that they would perceive me as a failure. So I went home that night and put on a brave front and acted as if nothing was wrong. That took all the strength I had. I got up the next day as if I was going to work. I got dressed and didn't alter my morning routine. I left the house and went to a shopping mall near my office and wandered around. I bought an ice-cream cone and sat on a bench in the mall and watched all the people going by. I felt so jealous of them as I watched them shop seemingly without a care in the world. How could the world go on for others when my world had just collapsed? I kept up this charade for a week and a half. My wife couldn't understand why I was unable to have sex with her and why I was so irritable with the kids. I knew that I had to do something. I couldn't keep up the facade. On the following Friday night when I came home 'from work' my wife told me about a beautiful new expensive piece of furniture she bought for our daughter's room. That was it! I blew up, blew my cover, and almost blew my marriage.

"At first my wife was incredibly hurt that I had kept this from her. She couldn't understand how I didn't share this with her. It was rough. We finally worked through that breach of trust, as she called it, and I felt incredibly re-lieved. I was finally able to express my emotions. I remem-ber crying as she held me tight. We talked for hours. That weekend we told the children that, 'Daddy lost his job. He feels sad about it, but he is going to look for a new and better job.' We told the children together, and both reas-sured them that we loved them and everything would be fine. The children were wonderful. After asking some ques-tions, they were very supportive. I nearly cried the next day when our daughter offered to sell her dolls to help out.

"After that, I decided to get started on my job search. (If I ever saw a mall again it would be too soon!) My wife helped me in my efforts and it was wonderful to be around my children more often. Within ten months, after many ups and downs, I had a new job that I was excited about. Looking back, I don't know how I would have managed without the support, understanding, and love from my family."

~

"Our chief want in life is somebody who will make us do what we can."
—RALPH WALDO EMERSON

Then there is the story of Hank R. He was divorced and his teenage son lived with his ex-wife, but Hank and his son would get together once a week. When Hank lost his job, he didn't tell his son. However, in the course of spending time together, his son realized that something was very wrong. A few months later he confronted his dad and asked him what was wrong. Hank told his son that he had lost his job a few months ago. His son was quite upset. He asked his dad how he would feel if he found out that his son was in trouble and hadn't told him, leaving Hank without the opportunity to show support or help his son. He said to his father,"That's how I feel now." Hank broke down on the spot and cried and knew that his son was right.

As we saw in Chapter 1, being fired is a major emotional trauma. It can be as important an event in your life as divorce, illness, and other major life crises. Your family will want to be there for you to help you through in whatever way they can. Declare the truth right away and ask for their support. For instance, they can assist you in your job search by helping you with researching companies, making telephone calls, doing mailings, setting up appointments, taking telephone messages, answering letters, identifying job leads, networking with their contacts, looking out for you, keeping you on track, cheerleading, disciplining, and most of all, giving you lots of love and moral support. There will be times when you will need lots of "rah rah" support, and other times when you will need a good swift kick in the behind. Sometimes you will welcome the cheerleading, while other times you may be feeling particularly defensive, and may push others away. Your family may wonder when to rally around you and when to back off, without being pushy or seeming indifferent, unsupportive, or appearing to abandon you in your time of need.

Because of the comfort level you usually feel with your family, they tend to see your worst side. Your family is often the scapegoat for the disappointment, hurt, frustration, resentment, betrayal, and anger that you feel. Sometimes you will say some unkind things to your spouse or your children that you really don't mean. Try to ensure that your family understands where the negativity is coming from. The more your family understands the emotions you are experiencing, the more helpful and compassionate they will be. Be aware of your mood swings. Remember to say thank you and hug your spouse when you are up to it. Appreciation and hugs go a long, long way. After the initial shock and anger of being fired dissipates, try to keep your social life as normal as possible. Don't withdraw into a shell. You will only feel worse and further isolated. Continue to go to church, to PTA meetings, to your weekly bridge games, etc. If the topic of your job comes up in conversation with acquaintances and neighbours, don't feel humiliated. Answer in a straightforward and positive manner. Job loss is becoming a fact of life. Discuss it openly and objectively. Leave the bitterness and anger at home. Don't forget, any conversation is a chance to network. Also, take time off for you and your partner together away from home. See a movie. Take your mind off your problems. Get away for a weekend. Go to dinner. You will both need this break from the pressure and a chance to enjoy each other. Also, take time alone to pursue your own interests and have a break from each other. Don't allow yourself to be overwhelmed and taken over by your job search and its pressure and strains. Make an effort to have some lighthearted fun.

Be prepared for a change in the family dynamics. Being home more will have both positive and negative effects on your family. When you are fired you have a feeling of loss of control. You have lost control over your destiny in your occupational setting. Sometimes, people will displace that need for control into the family situation and become more controlling than they otherwise would be. They may start to "manage" their family, and sometimes their management style won't work in a family setting! They will start to continually "lay down the law" in areas that they were not involved in before. This can cause a great deal of conflict, frustration, and disruption within the family. Be aware of this control displacement phenomenon and make sure you are not a culprit. If you recognize this as a problem, you may want to negotiate with your spouse and set limits on authority in different situations. Know who will set the rules for different cases. Then you will have a domain of control and you can work within those boundaries.If you lose your job and your spouse doesn't work, he or she may want to take a job to help out with the family finances. Or perhaps your spouse is already working. You may want to consider staying home and being a housewife or house-husband for a period of time. Being the primary care-giver will help you to structure your days by having a schedule to stick to and will help you to feel better about yourself for performing an important role in the family. Plus, you will be too busy to dwell on self-pity!

Michael F. has an interesting story to tell:

"I had been working as a Marketing Director for a theme park for four years. I had consistently received good performance reviews and I had the support of the Board of Directors. Then a new Chairman of the Board was appointed. She made it clear that she was not happy with present management. I guess I should have seen the writing on the wall, but I was shocked when I got called into the General Manager's office on that fateful Friday and was informed that she had been told to 'negotiate my exit.' Those were the exact words. They remained indelibly burned in my brain. It's funny how I was shocked but not really surprised given the recent circumstances. On the one hand, I felt relieved that I would not have to deal with this new Chairman who was hostile to management and, in addition to that, one of my close friends and allies on the management team had resigned and I was left feeling vulnerable. Yet, on the other hand, being fired is one of the worst experiences to go through. I guess you are never really prepared to hear those words.

"When it happened I came home and immediately told my wife. She was incredibly supportive. Then we told the kids, who were four and ten at the time. I initially told them that I had decided to leave the corporation, but as I got more comfortable with what happened, I told them that I had really been fired. Kids tend to take sides and see things in black and white. The corporation became the enemy and I was right. They were great. Also, because my job was a seven-day-a-week job (especially in the summers), my kids were happy that I would be home on the weekends and be able to spend more time with them.

"I was fired on the Friday of a long weekend and I had made plans with my father to go hunting in Northern Ontario that weekend. I was lucky that I got to spend time with someone whose opinions I value and who could put things in better perspective for me. I remember he told me that when one door closes, another one opens somewhere else. My father was great to talk to, and when I came back from that weekend with him, I felt better. It is really important to have people you can rely on. Being fired is so emotionally damaging to your ego. It is difficult to come to terms with it.

"I immediately met with a lawyer (whom I knew and trusted) upon my return. My lawyer then negotiated with the corporation. The negotiations became very protracted and messy. The process took over seven months and culminated in a very satisfactory settlement, but it also involved legal action which was very difficult. In fact, during the negotiation process, I heard back from my old staff that there were some uncomplimentary things being said about me at the corporation, and then articles started appearing in the press which disparaged the management of the corporation. I got very upset and began to worry if that would be damaging to my efforts at finding re-employment. There I was, trying to put a painful experience behind me, and begin a new working relationship in a negative climate that kept screaming at me in public and pulling me back.

"After I got fired, I took two weeks off and got my head on straight. Then my wife, who previously didn't work, decided to go into real estate. She went out to establish her career, and I stayed at home and became Mr. Mom. It gave me a routine to follow everyday. I did the housework, dropped off and picked up the kids, met my neighbours, and established a regular exercise routine. I had decided to get myself really fit — physically and emotionally. It was therapeutic to have a routine and soon I started to feel better about myself. After about three weeks, I started to work on my résumé, got the word out that I was back, and really began my job search in earnest. My job search then also became a very important part of my regular routine.

"One of the most difficult things that I had to deal with was the experience of being abandoned by my 'friends' and ex-colleagues. I found out who my real friends were and the backbone (or lack of it) in the people I had worked so closely with for the previous four years. I sure learned what that old saying 'A friend in need is a friend indeed' really means.

"It took about eight months to find a new job, and during that time there was a messy, negative, difficult lawsuit going on. It was a very tough time in my life. It really helped to have a lawyer that I trusted and a rigorous, regular routine. That kept me going. I also had a goal — I knew what I wanted, and had a plan to get it. What meant the most to me though, was to have the support of my wife and my kids. Especially on really bad days, it made all the difference to have someone there to put things in perspective for me. Now, looking back, I can truly say that although I went through a trauma, my life has been better for it. I moved on to a more suitable job for me which allows me to spend more time with my family, and this crisis has brought my wife and I much closer than we were before."

~

One of the great things about unemployment (yes there are advantages as we will see) is that you have the opportunity to become more involved with and closer to your children.

"Sweet are the uses of adversity; which like the ugly and venomous, wears yet a precious jewel in his head."
—WILLIAM SHAKESPEARE, *As You Like It*

What Do I Tell The Kids?

Children of all ages are sensitive to changes in family dynamics. They can sense when there is stress in the family. Young children need predictability, stability, routine, and continuity in their lives. They need a lot of comfort and reassurance to make them feel safe and secure during times of stress. When a parent is fired, young children will sense that something is wrong, and they may have a hard time differentiating a problem in the family from their role in causing it. Unless the job loss is explained to them in a simple, positive way, young children may feel that they are responsible for the tension and uneasiness in the home, and they may start to feel guilty and worry that they have done something wrong. You must explain what has happened to your children in an open, honest, upbeat way that they can understand. For example, you may want to say something like: "Daddy/Mommy has lost his/her job and will be home for awhile. He/she is not feeling very good about it, but it has nothing to do with you.

Daddy/Mommy is going to look for a new job. Everything is fine and Daddy and Mommy both still love you very much."

Children as young as three years old are able to grasp the general idea. They may not understand all of the complexities of the situation, but they understand that "Daddy lost his job and there will be less money coming in." There are some very heartwarming stories of how very young children have shown their support for the parent who was fired. Here are just a few:

- Sammy, upon hearing that his daddy lost his job, went upstairs to his room, broke his piggy bank, and came downstairs to give daddy his life's savings.

- David decided to go and get a paper route to help the family when his dad was laid off.

- Susan clipped all sorts of "neat" jobs out of the newspaper for her mommy when she got fired.

Be united with your spouse in terms of telling your children. Discuss what you will say to them in advance and tell them together. Then let your children tell you how they feel. Children will initially go through shock and disbelief. "How can they do this to Dad?" "Why?" Once they accept the situation, they will take their reactive cues from you and your spouse. If you are negative, they will be frightened. If you are positive, they will feel better and will usually want to help. It is a good idea to discuss with your children what they will say to their friends. Make sure your child understands and is comfortable with what they will say to others in response to questions about your new circumstances. It is important to reassure children. Their anxiety can be very real and they may have questions that they are afraid to ask. They may agonize over things for days before they finally bring themselves to ask the question that has been on their minds. For example, seven-year-old Billie wanted to know exactly when the money will run out. Five-year-old Jennifer wanted to know if there would be enough money to buy more peanut butter when the jar is empty. Nine-year-old Stevie wore shoes that hurt his feet and didn't tell anyone, because he didn't think they could afford to buy him new shoes. Try to answer your children's questions as specifically and honestly as you can, and try to always couch your answers in the positive. Never be alarmist with your children. They are very aware and sensitive to your feelings. They will pick up on your mood. If you are demoralized they will feel it and they will feel bad. If your activity level and mood picks up, they will feel that too. They also like to know what you did during the day. Keep them up to date on, and involved in, your job search. Share the ups with them and be as honest as is appropriate about the downs.

You and your spouse may have to decide on whether or not your children can continue with lessons (for example, dance or music lessons), or whether you will be able to send them to summer camp. There is a balance between trying not to disrupt the lives of your children, and putting undue added stress and hardship on you, your spouse, and the family unit. (If you are a single parent, you will have additional pressure on you. You must be strong for your children. They will need a lot of reassurance that their world will not fall apart. Make sure that you are getting enough support for yourself, so you will have the fortitude to be supportive and comforting to your children.)

Older children will need to know more information and specifics. Adolescents have more developed coping mechanisms for dealing with reality. They can separate the problem from their role in it. They can see that they are not responsible for the stress in the family, but they will want to know what is wrong. Older children can also help out in the home by looking after their younger siblings and helping with the household chores. Many kids have washed cars, mowed lawns, and done other odd jobs around the house to help out. Others have worked at part-time jobs to pay for their own purchases or contribute to the family coffers. Older kids can also help by networking with their friends' parents, or if they are adult with their own friends for you. You never know what could come from those leads.

Reality is such that some children will be more supportive than others. Some may even be resentful. Try not to let that hurt you. It is very important not to hide reality from your older children. In the process, they will be learning valuable lessons about life. They will learn to contribute, be responsible, and be aware that life is full of ups and downs.

> *"We learn simply by the exposure of living . . .*
> *The fact is we are being educated when we*
> *know it least. "*
>
> — David P. Gardner

The Pink Slip And The Single Executive

If you are single and you've lost your job, you may have to search a little further than your own backyard to find the emotional support that you will need. (However, the bright side is that you only have to worry about financially supporting yourself and not anyone else.) (A note here: if you are separated or divorced and must pay support payments, you may want to try to renegotiate your deal with your ex.) Upon being told the devastating news, you may be handed over immediately to your outplacement counsellor. If that is the case, you are lucky. Spend time with that person. Talk with them. Let out all your feelings. Express yourself. The outplacement counsellor is trained in this field and has the expertise to be able to help you. The counsellor will allow you to work through your initial emotions and prepare you to start to deal with your new reality.

If you don't have the benefit of a relocation counsellor upon termination, don't go home, lock yourself in your apartment and feel like you want to die. Don't disappear and withdraw from the world. That is one of the worst things that you could do. Don't try to deal with this trauma on your own. Go see or call your parents or your brothers or sisters. Tap into your family support system. If you don't feel comfortable with that, or it is not a possibility, call or go to see your closest friend(s). Lean on them for support. Remember, being fired is just like a divorce. You will need emotional support to get through this time of personal crisis. Of course you will need some time alone to mourn your loss, but don't close yourself off and isolate yourself from those closest to you. You will need their help. Like all times of great pain, you will have to reach deep inside yourself and find your internal strength and pull yourself out of this.

During the first few weeks after you've lost your job, when the anger and hostility is at its strongest and most fresh, you should limit your social contacts to your closest friends and your family. You don't want to put yourself in a position to say things you may later regret, burn bridges, or otherwise hurt yourself. People tend to run away from hostility. They don't know how to deal with it, and that can put a great deal of strain on an average friendship. After that initial intense stage, touch base and seek support from your friends. However, make sure you are selective in who you turn to for support. Choose people you know are strong and supportive and who will have it in them to give you that something extra. Avoid like the plague people who are apt to say, "Well, you think you're going through a rough time, listen to what happened to me. . ." Talking to these sorts of "friends" will be frustrating and fruitless.

Some well-meaning friends, relatives, or neighbours will sometimes say things that are debilitating and hurtful to you such as, "You haven't gotten a job *yet?*", or If *you* can't get a job it must be really bad out there!", or "Why not just take any job? At least you'll be working." Such comments are not only difficult to handle but are very disheartening. Explain to them that you will inform them if anything changes with regard to your job search, and you'd rather not discuss it further. If they still persist, either let these comments go right over your head, like water off a duck's back, or withdraw from that relationship. Also, realize that some days (or weeks) you may feel particularly down, and you won't be able to do much. This is to be expected. Don't feel guilty. You don't have to justify yourself to these people.

You may want to seek additional support through professional help such as doctors, psychologists, social workers, outplacement counsellors, or your local YMCA. You may feel cut off from your social circle as many of your friends may also have been your colleagues. It is human nature for people to be nervous about how to behave or what to say when a person has had a loss (job, divorce, death, etc.). Therefore, many of your friends and colleagues may feel uncomfortable and embarrassed around you. They may not understand these emotions and they may try to avoid that uncomfortable situation. It is not that they don't care or don't want to help. They just don't know what to do or what to say. Some friends may not call you right away out of respect and concern for your privacy. They may desperately want to be there for you, but just don't know how to open up the conversation, or they may fear your response.

Very often the best way to deal with this phenomenon is for you to approach your friends and say something like: "Look, I've been fired, and yes it is tough. I may need your help and support, but really I'm fine." Once you've admitted what happened and stated that you are alright, people will feel able to rally around you and will feel more comfortable about an inherently uncomfortable situation. On the other hand, if you appear as though you are about to fall apart and shy away from the topic or people, then you are closing the door to help from others. People will not be responsive to you. It is really important to lean on your friends and extended family for support. Do not try to be a solo soldier and go it alone. Find good listeners and peo-

ple that truly care and whose advise you respect. Then
talk to them and listen to them.

Ron A.'s story illustrates the importance of friends and
their support during unemployment (especially in the face
of less-than-understanding parents).

"I've been unemployed twice. The first time was August
6, 1980. It happened at 11:33 in the morning. I was the
Promotion Director at a radio station. My boss called me
into his office and told me that they were making changes in
the promotion department and there would be no room for
me. That's it! I was given no other reason! (I later painfully
found out that one of the higher-ups just didn't like me.) I
was stunned. Absolutely stunned, because nothing had ever
gone wrong. I was given fifteen minutes to leave the
premises. I went back to my office and slammed the door so
hard that when I went to leave, the door had jammed! I had
to call maintenance to get me out of my office! I had a little
emotional breakdown and went around the office and said
good-bye to all my friends and colleagues. There were a lot
of tears shed. I was there four and a half years and they gave
me three weeks severance pay! At the time I was too scared
and numb to do anything about it.

"Before I left the office, my telephone rang. It was a
friend of mine who worked at a movie company. She asked
me, 'What's new?' and I told her that I'd just been fired. She
immediately invited me down to her office. She brought me
a drink and showed me a movie in the screening room.
Then I went home. I couldn't stop thinking about what just
happened. I couldn't understand why they did this to me, or
what I did wrong. I felt useless and worthless, and I felt that
I would never work again. I drank a lot, smoked a lot, and
gained fifty pounds during a six-month period. I found out
that the person who didn't like me at my old job was saying
very nasty things and telling lies about me. This caused me
a great deal of trouble because the industry is small and
word travels fast. Employers were afraid to touch me. It was
devastating. My friends were what saved me. I kept in touch

with my key friends and contacts and they were wonderful and incredibly supportive. They took me to lunch and tried to keep me up to date on what was happening in the industry and where there might be potential job leads. They kept reassuring me that I was good at what I did. I needed to hear that so much. They were my life-line.

"I sent my résumé everywhere. I blindly searched for any job. After six months of unemployment I interviewed with a transportation company. They thought I was amusing and didn't quite understand me, but they hired me as their Regional Promotion Director. I soon realized that the job was wrong for me and ultimately it didn't work out. After two years of employment there, I was set up for the kill and was told that I would never go anywhere within the company. I left. This time I was unemployed for almost ten months. Again, I interviewed everywhere from theatres to banks to no avail. Was this a pattern? Deep down I knew that I am good at what I do. People kept telling me that I'm good. So why was I not working — again — and why were other people who are not so good at what they do employed? It became very hard to understand. I ballooned again and I felt useless and totally neurotic and insecure. I started to hang on every ad in the newspaper that was even remotely related to what I did. My parents kept telling me not to get excited or get my hopes up. I needed that hope, and my parents effectively depressed me. (I know that they meant well.) I started to wonder if I would have to give up my dreams and end up selling watches at a department store or being a box boy at the grocery store. What kept me going was a deep-seated belief in myself. I knew that I was good and that some day (hopefully soon) that would have to be recognized by somebody in a hiring position.

"I met with some headhunters and got offered a job with one of those firms to start up a new division to place promotion and public relations people. I did not want to make another career mistake, so over the next six weeks I met with everyone at that firm and did a lot of research into what the company was like and what the job would entail.

Much to my parents' chagrin, I realized that that job was not for me. Although I would be making astronomical money, it became clear to me that I was not a good fit with that firm: everyone there was motivated by one thing — money. I, on the other hand (though I love money), am chiefly motivated by creativity and the satisfaction of completing a successful project. I turned down that job in the face of much parental pressure to accept it. ("What, are you CRAZY to turn down that kind of money, especially when you have nothing else?!")

"I realized that I had to get focused in terms of my job search and concentrate on companies in the entertainment industry. One of my contacts told me about a job opening at a radio station. I applied for the job and got it. The station, the company, and the job are a perfect fit with my personality, talents, and work style. I have never been so happy in any job and I am very successful in my work and I am recognized for it. The company is generous with their praise and rewards. The right job was worth waiting for.

"What pulled me through and kept me going were my friends and contacts. Networking and shmoozing were the keys to my job search success. Someone once told me that when you leave a job there is something better waiting for you. It may take one month or two years to find it (it may not even be your next job, it may be the job after that), but you will find it. You must believe in yourself and have patience and persistence.

"What time has proven to me, is that what goes around comes around. I'm not really a religious person, but I think that what I went through was a test and a learning experience for me, and there was a pay-off at the end of the rainbow, which is where I'm sitting now. To a degree . . . I'm not totally there yet, but I'm on my way. My goal is to work in Hollywood and I have a target of three companies that I want to work for. Now I believe that it will happen. I fully expect to achieve my goal. But for now, I'm happy enjoying my job."

"Heaven is not to be won by rest and ease and quiet. Only those who have suffered and endured greatly have achieved greatly."
— ALFRED ADLER

Unfortunately, it is a fact of life that when the going gets tough, marginal friends get going. It is only when you go through a crisis that you find out who your true friends really are. Some of your friends will stick by you and support you, others will not. You will be surprised at who filters out. In the end, it is a valuable learning experience and the friendships that stay are strong and lasting. Also, you may want to consider joining a support group. Support groups can be a wonderful source of new and meaningful friendships. A note of caution here however, make sure that the support group you choose is not merely a self-pity group. It should be positive and helpful to its members (such as the group E.A.R.N. highlighted in Chapter 1).

After the initial shock created by job loss is over, it is important to maintain your outside activities. When you experience a major loss, it is a good idea to try to keep everything else in your life as stable as possible. Keep busy and most of all continue your social life. Get out and about. It will help to alleviate stress, will keep you upbeat, and you may even have a good time! However, you may feel that you are not ready to thrust yourself into a social situation. You may have a need to protect yourself from the added stresses these situations bring. Don't be overprotective with yourself. Don't stay away from social situations too long. You may have to push yourself, but get out there.

Another key reason for not avoiding social gatherings where you can meet people is the opportunity to network. Any social situation can involve a conversation which may lead to a job opportunity. If you are hiding at home crying into your pillow, you are missing important networking opportunities. Therefore continue to go to your trade association meetings, parties, dinners, luncheons, the fitness club, and anywhere else you enjoy going. It is estimated that over 80% of middle to senior management positions are not advertised. They are filled through the hidden job market. So get out there and meet and greet and sell yourself, sell yourself, sell yourself!

"And What Do You Do For A Living?"

Putting yourself in situations where you are meeting new people will invariably lead to that question: "And what do you do for a living?" This is one of the most feared, ominous questions if you've been fired, and one that is sure to come up within the first three sentences of conversation when meeting someone new. What do you do?

a) Panic.
b) Lie.
c) Change the subject.
d) None of the above.

Don't let the fear of this question make you avoid social gatherings. In response to this question, *do not* lower your head in shame, slump your shoulders, look down, and say in a quiet timid voice, "Nothing. I've been fired. I'm a total loser. In fact, I don't even know why you would want to waste your time talking to little old me."
Wrong, wrong, wrong!
Instead, a more appropriate response would be to stand erect, shoulders back and with your head held high, look the inquiring one right in the eyes and say in a strong voice, "I'm currently managing my career change,"or "I've decided to take some time off from the rat race and do things for myself, re-evaluate my priorities and values and check if I'm on track, or "I am an accountant (or whatever is appropriate) looking for a new setting. Do you know of any companies in need of my services?", or "I have been laid off and I am currently seeking employment in the XYZ field. Do you happen to know anyone who may be

able to help me or anyone that I could talk to in pursuing this path?"

The latter two responses are preferable because they open up the door for that person to help you. Know what you are going to say in response to this question in advance and practice saying the answer to yourself until you feel comfortable with it.

Always be honest. Always talk about your circumstances in a positive manner. This could be the first step in getting your new job. You never know who knows who and how they may be able to help you. Don't blow the chance to present yourself in the best possible light each and every time. And remember:

You never get a second chance
to make a first impression!

How Can I Face Mom And Dad?

A quick note on parents here. They grew up and lived in a world where if you worked hard, did a good job, and were loyal to your company, job security was your reward. If you were fired back then there was a real and negative stigma attached to it. That is their world — not yours. Times have changed. That is a very outdated belief system. Educate your parents as to the economic conditions you face today. It is no longer shameful or embarrassing to lose your job. Most parents will understand. It is very rare that your parents will ever consider you a failure. Most parents will offer support emotionally and/or financially. Appreciate it and accept it. There is no shame in accepting help when you need it.

Perhaps your parents are quite old and ailing and you don't want to burden them. Being there for you may give them a sense of being needed again. This is an invigorating feeling. Most parents will understand that the dynamics of the working world have changed. They may even know someone who knows someone . . . Get the picture? If you do not tell your parents and they find out, which they inevitably will (unless they live in a far away country), they will feel betrayed, hurt, and disappointed. If you still decide not to tell your parents and hope to get another job before you would need to tell them, recognize that you are taking a gamble. It is, of course, your decision, but take these factors into consideration. Don't let your pride end up hurting you. You are in control of the decisions you make. Don't let circumstances overcome you and cloud your judgement. Try to think clearly and make the best choices for you.

> *"Anxiety grows on solitude. Aloneness is the greatest breeding ground for the diffuse, unfocused, pervading uneasiness that makes us vulnerable to chronic worry."*
>
> — ALLAN FROMME

CHAPTER 3...

Why Me?

That's Life

"Men are disturbed not by things that happen, but by their opinion of the things that happen."

— EPICTETUS

Life is tough sometimes. In fact, life can seem brutal, cruel, and unfair at times.That is part of living. Everyone, no matter who they are, must come face to face with adversity and hardship in their lives. Why is it then, that although everyone has problems, some people are destroyed by life's difficulties, while others seem to become stronger as they conquer the challenges that face them? What causes one person upon being fired to jump off the roof of their expensive condominium, while his next-door neighbour upon learning of the same circumstance, becomes an even greater success?

The difference is how we perceive, interpret, and respond to events that occur in our lives. Do you let circumstances devastate you or do you see these painful experiences as opportunities to learn and grow? How you deal with life's obstacles determines to a great extent what you become in life and the happiness and fulfillment you enjoy (or don't enjoy). How you communicate to yourself about the adversity facing you determines how you feel, what you think, and how you behave.

Someone once said that it's not the hand of cards we get dealt that determines our happiness and success in life, it is how we play our hand that matters. In other words, you may not have control over all the circumstances or events that happen in your life; but you do have control of your reaction to and perception of these events. This means that your life is not out of control. You are your own master.

You have the power within you to overcome any problem that life throws your way. You do not have to be overwhelmed and devastated by the loss of your job. You can use this negative experience and turn it into a positive, learning and growing time in your life. What you need to be able to do is learn to control your state of mind; you need to be able to feel good in the midst of all your problems. Life is hard enough, you do not have to make it worse by feeling bad. Stuff happens. It's how you react to the "stuff" that dictates how well you will cope with life. You can drown in your troubles, or you can conquer them and like a surfer riding the crest of a wave be propelled by it and ride it to a great victory. It all depends on how well you are able to manage your emotions and how you perceive life's road blocks.

You can see your job loss as a failure and dwell on it and be afraid to move forward, or you can see it as an opportunity to get better. Don't be defeated by "failure." Failure is a learning experience and a way to get back on track. It is an outcome. That's all. You can put a negative value judgement on it, or not. It's up to you. When you were a baby and you were learning to walk you fell many, many times. You didn't know enough then to define that as failure, so you didn't stop trying. You learned from each fall you made how to balance yourself better and how to deal with this thing called gravity. You tried until you walked. That is why you walk today.

"Failure is the opportunity to begin again more intelligently."
— HENRY FORD

There are many people who overcame incredible odds and numerous setbacks, tragedies, and rejections to become some of the great successes of our time. For example, did you know that Abraham Lincoln failed in business twice, had his sweetheart die, suffered a nervous breakdown, lost numerous congressional and senatorial races before he was elected President of the United States and became remembered as one of the greatest leaders of modern times.

There was a Colonel named Sanders who at age sixty-five received his first social security cheque and realized that it wasn't enough for him to live on. He didn't have much to go on, he certainly was not young, yet he believed he had something of value in his chicken recipe. He drove all over the country trying to sell his chicken recipe. He was repeatedly rejected. He refined his approach and tried again and again and again. He got over a thousand rejections before someone finally said yes! If he had not kept persevering and if he hadn't viewed every rejection as an outcome instead of as a failure, we wouldn't have Kentucky Fried Chicken today.

> *"Nothing in the world will take the place of persistence. Talent will not; nothing is more common than unsuccessful men with talent. Genius will not; unrewarded genius is almost a proverb. Education will not; the world is full of educated derelicts. Persistence and determination are omnipotent."*
>
> — Calvin Coolidge

Thomas Edison was kicked out of school. He had his laboratory burn down. He had no insurance and lost everything. He tried thousands of filaments before he found the one that worked, but when he did he discovered the light bulb. When asked if he was not discouraged by all his failed attempts, his response was, "I didn't fail. I just learned thousands of ways not to make a light bulb."

Candy Lightner faced a parent's worst nightmare. She lost her young daughter when she was killed by a drunk driver. Candy could have been destroyed by this tragedy. Instead she chose to make her daughter's death mean something. She wanted to help others learn from her bitter experience. She founded the group Mothers Against Drunk Driving (MADD). Other lives have been saved because she was able to find a positive way of dealing with her fate.

There are also uninspiring stories of people who were unable to manage their emotions and who couldn't see themselves in a positive light no matter how much evidence there was to the contrary. People like Elvis Presley, Marilyn Monroe, and Freddie Prinze could not learn to control their states. They tried to change how they felt by altering their states with drugs and alcohol. It didn't work to their satisfaction. They were all loved, talented, and wealthy. They seemed to "have it all," yet it was never enough because they could never truly reach the state they desired the most. They could never feel happy within themselves. Life overcame them.

"The measure of mental health is the disposition to find good everywhere."
— Ralph Waldo Emerson

The key to unlock the treasure chest of happiness and success in your life is to know how to control the way you feel. Feeling positive (even when faced with dire circumstances) will pull you through anything. When you feel good you will behave in a positive manner, and positive behaviour will get good results. People see you as you see yourself. Be up on yourself and people will be up on you. The question is, how do you control the way you feel? How can you triumph over negative emotions? There are two ways:

1. Manage and control what you think and say to yourself.

2. Manipulate and master your physiology (that is, your body movements, voice, breathing, etc.).

It's All In Your Mind

*"In the province of the mind, what we believe
to be true either is true or becomes true."*
— JOHN LILLY

Your thoughts have incredible power. What you say to
yourself can either empower you or cripple you. Thoughts
can be real forces. Your beliefs can actually be self-fulfill-
ing prophecies. You can fill your mind up with negative,
self-defeating thoughts, or you can let positive, empowering thoughts engulf your mind. It is your choice. You can
replace thoughts of insecurity, worthlessness, and self-
doubt with thoughts of confidence, success, and self-
worth. Don't let yourself feel inferior or inadequate.
Instead, take charge of your mind, your thoughts, and
your feelings *now!*
    For example, you may be thinking things such as:
"Why did this happen to me?"
"I'm a failure."
"I'm worthless."
"I really screwed up."
"Life stinks."
"Life is so unfair."
"I'll never get another job again."
"I'm all washed up."
"I'm a fraud and now everyone knows it."
"I'm a loser."
"I feel lousy."
"I can't do it."
"I give up."
"I'm not up to it today. Maybe tomorrow."
"What's the use?"
"It won't work anyway."
Do any of these thoughts sound familiar? You don't have
to further batter your self-esteem. These self-destructive
thoughts will not help you. Take responsibility and control

what thoughts occupy your mind. Next time you feel a negative thought coming into your mind, consciously push it out and replace it with thoughts that will help you build back up your self-esteem and make you feel better. Always try to be aware of what you say to yourself. For example, if you are going for a job interview, don't say things to yourself like "Why will this interview be different? I know that I won't get the job anyway, so why even bother?" This will come across in your communication to the interviewer. Instead you can think to yourself something like "I feel great! I know that I'll do well in this interview. I feel very confident about my abilities." What you think about yourself will be communicated and will be reflected in what others think of you.

> *"They can because they think they can."*
> — VIRGIL

Here are some positive thoughts to say to yourself:
"I am a special person."
"I am worthwhile."
"I feel good about myself."
"I like and respect myself."
"I have many special capabilities and talents."
"I feel great today!"
"I am smart."
"I am confident."
"I am grateful for all I have and for who I am."
"I am enthusiastic about life."
"I feel energetic and full of vitality."
"I am happy."
"I am a winner."
"I am a success."
"Every day I'm getting better and better."
"I am in control of my life."
"I won't give up."
"I can do whatever I decide to do."

Initially, it will require a conscious effort to think these positive thoughts instead of the old comfy-cozy negative thoughts that you are used to. It will feel awkward and different. You may even feel that you are lying because you don't really feel great or any of those other things above. If you wait until you do feel great before you say those things to yourself, you could be waiting a very long time. Why not just speed up the process? You will be surprised at the effect continually thinking these thoughts will have. Soon it won't be such an effort to replace your negative thoughts with positive ones. Thinking empowering thoughts will start to come naturally, and then, lo and behold, you *will* start to feel better.

> *"We are never living, but only hoping to live; and looking forward always to being happy, it is inevitable that we are never so."*
>
> — PASCAL

It is helpful to say these positive thoughts aloud to yourself in addition to thinking them silently. It helps to keep your mind focused. Say them to yourself in the mirror when you brush your teeth every morning and every evening. Write them down on index cards and carry these cards with you and refer to them during the day. Record these thoughts on a cassette and play it in your car (this is a great way to alleviate tension while stuck in traffic). Another good exercise is to write down on a sheet of paper all the things that you like about yourself. Then take that sheet and put it somewhere visible (maybe on the fridge) where you can read it every day.

You will see a change in yourself. You will feel better and better. Use the power of your mind to master your feelings instead of letting your thoughts control you. People tend to become what they think about most. Make sure you become all you want to be. You are in the driver's seat.

The Answer Depends On The Question

"Happiness requires problems plus a mental attitude that is ready to meet distress with action toward a solution."

— H. C. HOLLINGWORTH

Your brain works like the most powerful computer in the world. If you ask it a question, your brain will search and search until it comes up with an answer. Therefore, you've got to be careful about what questions you ask yourself, because you may not like the answers you get. For example, if you continually ask yourself "Why did this happen to me? Why me? Why?" your brain will eventually come up with an answer: "Because you're a failure." "Because you're a loser." "Because you deserve it."

Neither the questions nor the answers have any basis in reality. That doesn't matter. What matters is what feels real to you, and this dialogue with yourself will not make you feel good at all. There is nothing to be gained by this line of questioning. Instead, you can ask yourself more suitable questions such as: "What can I learn from this?" "How can I grow from this?" "How can I become better because of this experience?" "What can I find to laugh about in this situation?"

Make a list of what you are happy about in your life, what you are proud of, and what you are grateful for. If you can't think of anything you are happy for, proud of, or grateful for, step back for a minute and think about it. You have your health. You live in a free country full of possibility. You have the opportunity to assess and evaluate your life. You have time to spend with the ones you love. You've accomplished a great deal in your life. I'm sure that you can think of all sorts of things if you try. If you are busy thinking about positive things, you won't have time to dwell on the negatives. What a pity! It really works. Try it. You won't be sorry.

"Most people are about as happy as they make up their minds to be."

— ABRAHAM LINCOLN

Is The Glass Half Empty Or Half Full?

When you look at this glass, if you are feeling lousy, you will probably say that the glass is half empty. If you are feeling great, you may say the glass is half full. Well, what is it: half empty or half full? The answer is, it depends on your perception. Your perception is your reality. For example, have you ever been involved in a car accident? When the police came to talk to the drivers involved and the witnesses, did you notice how no two people described the accident in the same way. Everyone had a different perception of what happened. Who is right? What then is reality?

Your reality is what you focus on and how you perceive things at the time. Let me give you another example. Pretend that you took a trip. You've decided to bring your video camera with you to tape it. It is impossible to shoot every single thing, as the camera can only focus on one thing at a time. Therefore you must miss some activities. When your vacation is over you will have your perception of your experience of your trip recorded. Perhaps you shot people begging for money or food, desolate places, or the ugliness of your hotel. You may think that your vacation was lousy. Perhaps you had a fight with your mate while away. You won't have good memories of your vacation and you will have your video tape to play over and over to confirm that the trip was awful. Now, suppose that your friend went on the same trip and also brought a video camera along. However, the scenes that were captured on that video were different. That video shows happy, joyful people, beautiful scenery, and the interesting architecture of the hotel. Also, suppose that your friend met a very special person on that trip. You can bet that your friend will think that it was a fabulous vacation. Who is right?

What you focus on and think about becomes your reality. How you feel also shapes your perceptions. For example, if you went to a party feeling sick or depressed would you have as good a time as you would if you went to that party feeling healthy, vibrant, and on top of the world? I don't think so.

When you feel good you tend to notice the positive things around you. It follows that when you feel bad, you tend to notice the negative things around you. Your experience of any situation depends on you. There is always both good and bad in life. Whether you choose to focus on the positive or the negative is also up to you.

"Reality is created by the mind. We can change our reality by changing our mind."

— PLATO

People are generally inclined to worry and to imagine the worst possible outcome of things. This is even more pronounced if you already feel poorly. The interesting thing is, however, that like a camera, you can only focus on one thing at a time. Therefore, if you are thinking self-defeating thoughts, you will tend to see the negative side of things and that will make you feel worse. Experiences themselves do not have inherent "meaning." You perceive events and then define them. Nothing really means anything until you define what it means to yourself. For example, losing your job doesn't mean that you are a failure. It could mean that you have been given a great opportunity to explore, expand, and re-evaluate your life. It all depends on your attitude. The way you think about yourself will determine what you do or do not do in life and how others see you. If you change how you think, you can change your attitude and therefore your destiny. Start to change how you think and talk now.

"Destiny is not a matter of chance, it is a matter of choice."

— UNKNOWN

Change:

I can't to I CAN!
I'll try to I WILL!
Remember, whether you feel you can or can't do something, you're absolutely right!

Was That My Imagination?

Another really interesting thing about your mind is that it can't tell the difference between a real experience and an imagined one. That has powerful implications for you. If you keep telling yourself over and over what a failure you are, your mind will eventually believe this to be true and will react accordingly. The opposite is also true. That is why repetition of positive thoughts is so important. If you have an important job interview coming up, you can vividly picture the interview in your mind going exactly the way you want it to go. Visualize your interview as specifically as you can. Picture yourself as confident and self-assured. You are answering all the questions well. You are calm and collected. As you leave the interview, you feel great because you know that you had a very productive meeting. You are a success! Rehearse phone calls in your mind the same way. Try to anticipate questions that will be asked and prepare your answers in advance. You will feel more comfortable in making the call. Always see yourself as confident and successful.

> *"Winners expect to win in advance. Life is a self-fulfilling prophecy."*
> — UNKNOWN

There have been experiments showing that mental practice will bring about the same results as real physical practice in darts and basketball. Athletes already know the power of mental exercise and use it as an essential part of their training process. Now you can tap into this wonderful force and increase your potential. Try improving your tennis game, or golf swing, or skiing, by picturing yourself hitting, swinging, or shooshing perfectly in your mind. It will make a big difference! Concentrate on and picture in your mind what you want, not what you don't want. For example, don't say "I don't want to fumble this interview." Instead say "I will handle this interview beautifully."

Another useful purpose your imagination can serve is to help you to relax. You can't feel anxious, angry, upset, or fearful if your muscles are totally relaxed. It is impossible. Here are some good relaxation exercises:

1. Imagine that your body is totally limp. Feel like a rag doll. Try to move and let parts of your body flop around.

2. Lie down on a bed, couch, or the floor. Imagine that your body in very, very heavy. Try to lift your arms or your legs. Feel how difficult it is.

3. Concentrate on isolating your muscles. Tighten and then release each muscle individually from the top of your head to the tips of your toes. Imagine your muscles as dominos, and as each one tightens and relaxes it falls down and proceeds to the next one. Feel the pressure and then the release of each part of your body.

4. Imagine yourself at your favourite peaceful place. You can picture yourself soaking up the sun on a beautiful beach; you can imagine that you are on the top of a mountain or by a serene stream. The point is to imagine yourself in a scene that is very relaxing to you. Try to picture things as vividly and in as much detail as possible. For example, if you decide to take yourself to a tropical paradise in your mind, feel the sun's heat beating down on your skin, hear the waves of the ocean crashing in, see the white sand, and the palm trees blowing gently in the breeze. Doesn't that feel great!

It is a good idea to try to relax before an important interview to wipe out any negative forces from your body and mind and go in with a clear, focused mind and a relaxed, energized body. It will make such a difference in how you feel and therefore how you behave and ultimately how you are perceived. Although it is not known exactly why or how your mind works this way, this shouldn't stop you from using this incredible tool. You may not understand exactly why or how your computer works, but you will turn on the switch and use it anyway. There is great power in your imagination. *Use it!*

Pump It Up

There is a very real connection between your body and your mind. What you think directly affects your body. (Do you remember seeing your "ex" for the first time and feeling that immediate sinking, sick feeling in your stomach?) It is well documented that stress can cause physical problems in the body. Your thoughts directly affect how you feel both physically and mentally, and therefore how you will behave. If you are feeling down on yourself, you may not feel well physically. You may be more susceptible to colds, flues, and all sorts of ailments. At the very least, you won't be an energetic, vibrant person. Because your body feels lousy, you won't feel well emotionally and so the endless loop goes on.

Depression is a good example of how the mind/body connection works. Depression is not a virus. You don't "catch" it. Whether you realize it or not, you have to work at feeling depressed. For example, your body must be a certain way.

ANATOMY OF A DEPRESSED PERSON

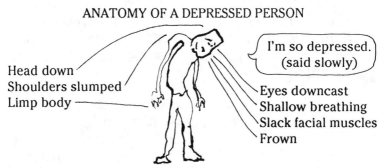

Head down
Shoulders slumped
Limp body

I'm so depressed.
(said slowly)

Eyes downcast
Shallow breathing
Slack facial muscles
Frown

Is this a familiar picture? If so, try this:

- LOOK UP
- STAND STRAIGHT
  (SHOULDERS BACK)
- TILT YOUR HEAD
  SLIGHTLY UP
- BREATHE DEEPLY
- SAY POSITIVE THINGS
- SPEAK WITH ENTHUSIASM
        AND
  SMILE!

I feel great!
(said with enthusiasm)

I'll bet you will feel much better.

Your body sends messages to your brain about how to feel by what it is doing. If you can maintain a positive physiology, you can feel good on cue. It sounds too simple to be true, but just try it. You'll see for yourself that it works. For example, when you smile, the muscles in your face send a different message to your brain about how to feel than when you frown. Smile, and see how before you know it, you do actually feel better and the world doesn't seem like such a dark place.

Every move that you make will have an impact on how you feel. Even the way you speak (how quickly and how loud you talk, your pitch, and voice inflections) will affect how you feel. So use your body in an empowering way. Don't let your body disempower you. If you want to feel wonderful, act that way. If you want to feel successful and confident, act that way. If you don't have it in you to do that, then at least act *as if* you were feeling successful and confident. Walk as you would if you were feeling totally confident. Talk as you would if you were feeling totally successful. Gesture as you would if you were feeling on top of the world. Breathe as you would if you were feeling great. Move and act as if you were feeling successful and confident and those messages will be sent to your brain and before you know it you will truly start to feel that way. Pump yourself up like this before every job interview. It will make you feel wonderful and that, as we know, will enable you to behave in a much more beneficial way.

This is an easy and wonderful tool to use. Remember, if you talk and act with enthusiasm and energy you will feel more alive and vibrant than you thought possible. If you control what you say and think to yourself you can make yourself feel great. Isn't that a better way to feel than how you're feeling now? Well, go ahead, change your mood. Use the power of your mind. Get up and strut your stuff. You've still got what it takes. In fact, you're even better now!

Ready, Set, Action!

"A journey of a thousand miles begins with the first step."

— CONFUCIOUS

The next key is what you do with the stuff you strut. A positive frame of mind will make you feel great, full of energy and motivated. The next step is taking *action.* It is important to have a plan. You can't get where you're going if you don't know how to get there or even worse, where it is you want to go; and you can't go anywhere without taking the steps to get there.

You must evaluate yourself (your values, beliefs, strengths, and weaknesses) and set goals for yourself. Positive thoughts, vivid visualization, and a powerful physiology will mean nothing if you don't have a plan of action and then act on that plan.

Although things in life rarely go exactly according to plan (as you have recently learned), having goals and working towards them will at least set you on the right road. We will cover self-examination and goal setting in Chapter 4. For now it is important to know that your mind and body are tools you can use to help you get yourself motivated. But that is not enough. You have got to get into high gear and work towards achieving what it is you want.

"Things may come to those who wait, but only the things left by those who hustle."

— ABRAHAM LINCOLN

It's Not What You Say, It's How You Say It

"Man's mind, once stretched by a new idea, never regains its original dimensions."

— OLIVER WENDALL HOLMES

In pursuit of your goals (one of which is obviously to get a job or become self-employed), you will find yourself in situations where how well you communicate to others will be a critical factor in your success in anything from having a winning interview to negotiating a loan from your bank. Good communication skills are very important in your ability to interact with others, your capability to get what you want, and therefore your capacity to live a more fulfilling life.

It is interesting to note that only 7% of communication is done by words; 38% of communication is tonality; and a whopping 55% of all communication is done by body language. Therefore, what you say, how you say it, and what your body says should all be in synch to produce clear communication. For example, if you are in an interview situation and you say "I know that I have the abilities to do this job well," and you say these words in a meek, quiet voice with hesitation between words, and you are looking at the floor, with a scared expression on your face, as you sit slumped in the chair — do you think that the interviewer will have faith in the words you said? Contrast that picture with candidate B, who says the same words but says them in a strong, secure voice, confidently looking the interviewer directly in the eyes, sitting straight up in the chair. If you were the interviewer who would you choose? If your body conveys conflicting signals than the words you say, the message of your body will dominate and that will become the meaning of your communication.

Words alone are meaningless. People will notice your body movements, gestures, eye contact, facial expressions, vocal pitch, tone and inflections, and even intangibles such as your level of confidence, your sense of humour, your comfort level within yourself, your level of commitment and stability, and much more. It all goes together to form a communication package, and it is your responsibility to make sure that the right package is delivered. It is up to you to make sure that the correct message gets through to the right person. It is not the listener's fault if they "don't get it." And remember that just as your perception is your reality, other people's perception of you is their reality. It is up to you to make sure they get a clear picture of what it is that you want them to see. That is why it is very important to go into an interview feeling confident and successful (or acting as if you feel confident and successful) because, without realizing it, you will behave and move in those ways and that part of your communication will be received.

It has been estimated that upon initial meetings, people form an impression of each other within the first *seven seconds!* Much of this sizing up is done instinctively. Have you ever had an experience where someone tells you something and you don't believe it, but you can't put your finger on exactly why? This is your mind processing the meaning of their communication in a non-verbal way versus the words they actually used, and something doesn't add up. The words are in conflict with the body. Therefore, try to feel inside what you are trying to convey on the outside. In this way your communication will be in synch, there will be synergy and you will successfully communicate in a powerful and direct way.

It will also help matters immensely if the person you are communicating with likes you. If you can establish rapport with someone, the communication process becomes easier and more fruitful. The question is, how do you establish rapport? People generally like other people that they feel are similar to themselves. So try to establish something in common with the person you are talking to. For example, you may have friends in common, similar interests or hobbies, you may both be the same religion, you may both have graduated from the same school, grew up in the same neighbourhood (or country if you are both foreigners), etc. You can look for these points in common and highlight them if they exist, but you have no control over these factors.

There are, however, certain ways to establish a common bond that are controllable. You can change your physiology to match theirs. For example, you can have the same body language, speech patterns, and behaviours as the person you are meeting with. How do you do this? Simple, you copy the other person! This is called mirroring. If you copy how someone is sitting, gesturing, breathing, moving, posturing, and the tone, pace, volume, and inflection of their speech, they will like you without knowing exactly why because mirroring works on a subconscious level. They will feel comfortable with you because you are similar to them. However, be careful not to be too obvious when mirroring. You don't want anyone to realize that you are copying them and become offended. If you are subtle in your approach usually they won't even notice. Mirroring works! Try it out. You'll see fabulous results.

Here are some tips for good, effective communication:

1. Be flexible in your communication approach. Look for points of similarity, and try to de-emphasize and diffuse any points of difference. Notice what is working or not working. If you are not getting the

response you want, change your communication approach.

2. Try not to use the word "but." It tends to negate what you said before it and makes the other person feel ignored. Substitute the word "and" in place of "but" and the person you are talking with will become less adversarial. For example, instead of saying "I see what you mean *but* I think . . ." say, "I see what you mean *and* I also feel that . . ." By this simple word replacement, the person you are communicating with will feel that their point of view was heard and that will generate a feeling of mutual respect. This will allow for the possibility of positive realignment of the conversation back to common ground where it can be more productive.

3. Try to find the humour in tense situations. It can be a great ice-breaker and can diffuse even the worst circumstances.

4. Talk less and listen more. You learn much more by listening, and when you listen, be sure to hear what is being said. Don't fidget or think about what you're going to say next, or what you're going to have for dinner, or how the interviewer's hair looks like a toupee. Focus your mind and concentrate on *listening* to the other person.

5. Think before you react. This will give you time to cool down. It is usually a mistake to react emotionally. Try to remain calm and collected. Don't jump to conclusions or jump in and finish someone's sentences for them. Always let the other person finish their thought.

6. Notice the differences (or similarities) between what a person is saying and how they are saying it, and be aware of the same thing in yourself. Be congruent in your communications, and always be an

active participant. Be aware of what is going on at all levels and at all times.

7. Look the person in the eye. This does not mean that you should go overboard and try to win a staring contest; just try to maintain good eye contact.

8. Always be honest and act with integrity.

9. Be enthusiastic and smile. It's contagious.

Let's conclude this chapter with a look at how persistence, focusing, and feeling positive helped Harry P.:

"I have a Ph. D. in biochemistry and an M.B.A. I was raised in England and worked all over the world for large corporations in international marketing. I was at the forefront of biotechnology. I came to Canada as a vice-president of an international corporation with a mandate to handle a major acquisition. I succeeded; however, I did not click with the president of the subsidiary company, which resulted in my departure from the corporation. To be honest, I was ready to leave. I had been with the corporation for eleven years and I had gone about as far as I was going to go. I left with a generous financial package and I was already being pursued by another firm to handle a start-up company in the high technology field.

"I took their offer and signed a five-year contract at a salary of $100,000 per year, plus a 10% ownership in the company. The other 90% of the company was owned by a public company, the chairman of which guaranteed the financing of this start-up company for five years. I thought I was on a 'gravy train'! I started the company and developed new products, all according to the approved business plan. As it turned out, the parent company did not have sufficient cash flow to support this new venture, and the rug was pulled out from under my feet. I had to downsize the company from a staff of fifteen to three people overnight. It broke my heart. I knew that it was time to get off that 'gravy train.'

"I joined the ranks of the unemployed in May 1990. I was too arrogant at the time to apply for my unemployment insurance benefits. I started a company with my wife and we consulted to high tech small companies in search of a new direction. From May to September we had a few clients, but as the recession hit, the clients dried up. I also realized that I was better in a large corporate environment than in a small business venture. The only things that I enjoyed about running our small business were the flexibility it gave me and the freedom I had to play more with my infant daughter, which I never had as much time for with my other children.

"From September onward, I started a full-time campaign to look for another job. I targeted the biotechnology industry and wrote letters and sent résumés to these companies and wrote to headhunters in that field. Then I waited for the phone to ring. It didn't. I sent out approximately 450 resumes and letters and I got only two or three responses, all of which were negative. I wondered what I was doing wrong. I changed my letter three times and targeted venture capitalists who had connections with the biotechnology industry. I got the same response. I was obviously still doing something wrong. I kept changing my approach and trying again. I wouldn't give up. I had no alternative. By November, I was sending out ten to twenty customized letters each day and making follow-up calls to each one of them to no avail. I was getting progressively depressed. Christmas was fast approaching; we were broke and wondering how we were going to meet our mortgage payments. It was time to apply for my unemployment insurance benefits (which I had been an idiot not to apply for immediately).

"I felt very depressed. It seemed that everything around me was black. I was treating my family badly. I was unhappy with myself. I felt like I was in a Monopoly game and I was losing. I couldn't collect $200 when I passed Go because there was too much rent to pay and I was sliding faster and faster into losing the game. When I tried to talk to friends in social situations if the topic of my unemployment came up (which it invariably did), people became nervous about being around me. It was awful. I had to pull my son out of private school and I felt terrible about that. My nineteen-year-old daughter had to get a job and contribute to the household. I feel very lucky that I had such a supportive wife. She was my saving grace.

"One day in Novembe. my wife saw an article in the newspaper about a support group for unemployed executives and suggested that I give them a call. It took me until January to make that call. I was bored with continually writing letters that were generating lousy (if any) responses, and I thought that I might be able to learn how to market myself better through the group. I went to my first meeting and started to have fun right away. I met lots of great people and I came home from that first meeting feeling better (and again chastised myself for not calling sooner). I attended a résumé writing seminar (thinking that I had an excellent resume) and was surprised to learn what other people's perceptions were of it. I immediately changed my résumé. The group had a speaker come in who was an executive outplacement specialist. I was impressed, and I went to see him and negotiated a learn-now-pay-later agreement with him. He taught me how to market myself in the 1990s. (The last time I had to look for a job was twenty years ago. The world has sure changed.) I became more targeted and focused. I started to send out three to five letters and résumés a week, and made a few well-targeted cold calls and got positive responses to most of them.

"I also got more involved with the support group and got my act together. When I started doing things, getting involved and contributing to the group, I felt much more positive about myself and life started to look much brighter. I started to feel confident about myself and my ability to find re-employment. I stayed focused in my efforts and kept at it. It was funny, as I started to feel positive, positive things started happening to me. One day I saw an ad in the newspaper for a president of a large public corporation. I faxed my résumé in immediately, called them thirty minutes later, and I got an interview within the next forty-eight hours.

After numerous interviews, I was to meet with the Board of Directors. I made a presentation to them with a flip-chart and a ten-page document outlining potential strategies. The board was impressed, and I got the job! The company is only a fifteen-minute drive from home, the job is a higher level position than the one I left, and it pays a great deal of money.

"All in all, I sent out approximately 500 letters and résumés and made hundreds of calls in my job search. Things really started happening for me when I started to feel more positive, got focused, and targeted the right companies using the right approach. A large factor in my job search success was that I started to feel better about myself, and I started to see the light instead of the darkness. Good things and great opportunities came my way when I became more open to them. When I was doubled over with worry and despair I was closed off to my potential.

"Being unemployed was an important transition in my life. I learned a great deal about myself and how to interact with other people in a much more generous way than I had before. I've also lost my arrogance and become a lot more human. I've learned how to believe in myself and my goals in a much more positive way. Although it was a very rough time, I'm better for having gone through it."

~

"He who believes is strong; he who doubts is weak. Strong convictions precede great actions."

— J. F. CLARKE

CHAPTER 4...

Who Am I – Really?

I Can't Get No . . . Satisfaction

Everyone in life wants to be happy and feel fulfilled. What does that take? Well, unless you've recently won a lottery or are otherwise independently wealthy, you will spend a great deal of your life working. Therefore, if you enjoy what you do at work, if you like (or better yet, even love) your job, your chances of happiness will increase dramatically. You may think, that is all well and good; but right now you are just trying to get through each day. You are just trying to get another job as fast as you can. Happiness seems like a far-away dream.

Well, wake up and smell the coffee! You deserve to be happy. You can be happy. You will be happy.

How do I know this? Because you are going to take this opportunity that you have been given — yes, I'm talking about being fired as an opportunity again — as a time to pause, evaluate, reassess, and grow. Plan your life the way that you want to live it. Although times of transition are usually painful, they are also the times when you learn and develop the most. You learned about the importance of perspective in Chapter 3. Look at being fired in the proper perspective. Losing your job, although painful, forces you to take a break from the treadmill you were on and catapults you into a new world of the unknown.

How exciting! You have been given an opportunity to discover your natural talents and abilities, and to explore new pathways and arenas in which to best utilize and express the real you. Or you may confirm to yourself that you want to continue on the path that you were on, and this time of unemployment will be just a bump in that road, but you will have learned about yourself in the process.

Think of what would have happened to you if you hadn't lost your job. Close your eyes and imagine where the road you were on would have led. Where would you have been in five years? Doing what? Where would you have been in ten years? In twenty years? Would you have felt happy and fulfilled, or would you have regrets? Were you on a certain career path because when you were young you got an academic degree in it? Or because your parents wanted you to follow a certain direction and you didn't want to let them down? Or were you doing something for so long it was just expected of you? Or did you have too much to lose? You didn't want to give up security to follow a pipe dream. Have you ever really stopped to wonder if you were truly satisfied at your job?

Now is the time to take control of your life and direct your future so you will be on the right track to living a more meaningful, satisfying, and fulfilling life. This is a chance for you to get to know yourself better. Understand yourself more fully. Discover what makes you great. You are special. You are unique. You have within you unlimited potential! Don't set limits for yourself. Stretch yourself beyond what you thought you could ever do. You can achieve your dreams. In order to reach your full potential you must:

- *Know yourself — what you have to offer (and who needs it).*
- *Know what you want.*
- *Know how you are going to get there.*

> **"He who knows much about others may be learned, but he who understands himself is more intelligent. He who controls others may be powerful, but he who has mastered himself is mightier still."**
>
> — Lao-Tsu, Tao Teh King

To Thine Own Self Be True

> **"There is only one success — to be able to spend your life in your own way."**
>
> — Christopher Morley

How well do you think you know yourself? Do you have a perfectly clear understanding of your values, beliefs,

skills, talents, strengths, weaknesses, interests, and passions? Not many people do. You are one of the lucky ones
who have been given this opportunity to objectively evaluate yourself. However, make no mistake: the process of
getting to know yourself is not easy. It is hard to be objective. You may discover some things about yourself that
you don't like. This journey into self-discovery will take
courage, patience, endurance and most of all, real honesty
with yourself. However, when you reach your destination
of self-awareness, it will be worth the trip. You will have
gained valuable life and career insight by learning about
your real self. You will know what motivates you, what is
most important to you, what you are really good at, and
what type of environment you will flourish in versus what
type will cause you to shrivel up.

If you can conduct a focused and targeted job search
that is driven by a force within you, you will not only be
more successful in the search process; but you will also be
more satisfied in the job you end up getting. Remember
Ron's story in Chapter 2? He learned the hard way that
you must be a good fit with the company you work for and
be doing what you want to do to truly feel happy in your
job. He went through a wrong job fit and did not let himself make that same mistake twice. He knew what he was
good at, targeted an industry and certain companies
within that industry, and was ultimately successful in not
only his job search, but in his job as well.

It is like a marketing exercise: know your product
(you), know what it is and the needs it fills, know the target market (industries, companies, jobs), and how to most
effectively and efficiently communicate to that market.

If you get a job with a company that has values (corporate culture) that mesh with your values and you use your
abilities that motivate and energize you in fulfilling your
mandate, then you will most likely perform very well and
be happy at your job. The key then is finding the job that
is right for you. (It is just like finding the outfit that fits you
well and suits you best. It will highlight your best features

and diminish your weaknesses. Remember, any outfit may look good on a rack, but what matters is how it looks on you.)

Before you can identify the perfect fit, you must know who you are, what you would like to be, what you would like to do, and where you would like to do it. It is time to start the slow, hard process of your personal reassessment and self-evaluation.

"Winning starts at the beginning."

— ANONYMOUS

Journey Into Discovery
Values And Beliefs

"Man is what he believes."

— ANTON CHEKHOV

Your values are the core and centre of your self that help to define the direction that your life takes. Your values and beliefs work very closely together. First of all, your values are what you believe is right, wrong, good, and bad, and what is most important to you. Your values and beliefs are rooted deep within you and have been instilled in you early in childhood by your parents, teachers, and friends. They are molded by what you have been rewarded or punished for and continue to take root as you grow up. Some examples of values are:

honesty	commitment	independence
love	freedom	recognition
security	success	integrity
power	happiness	contribution
growth	family	achievement
honour	health	control

Each individual will have his or her own hierarchy of values. For example, some people will place power and success above honesty and integrity. Some people will place security above freedom. You will have your own list of values and their importance to you.

You also have your own set of beliefs. They are rules you set up to determine how you feel. For example, if you value success, how will you know if you are achieving it?

— If you make a great deal of money? If so, how much money do you need to make to feel that you are successful?

— If you are popular and respected? If so, how many people have to like and admire you? Everyone you meet? Your peers? Your industry leaders? Your boss?

— If you have achieved a certain title? If so, what title? C.E.O.? President? Vice-president? And by what age? By the time you're thirty? By age forty? Fifty?

Are your rules impossible to meet? Are your beliefs realistic, yet do they make you stretch? What you believe will determine your perspective (and you are now well aware of the importance of a good, positive perspective). For example, what do you believe about life? Is it a challenge? Does it stink? Is it fair? Is life wonderful?

What do you believe about people? Are they inherently dishonest or honest? Are they always looking for ways to help you or cut you down? Are they always looking out for themselves or do they generally care about others?

What do you believe about yourself? (Check back to Chapter 3 if you come up with negative self-talk here!)

Remember, that just as the beliefs you have about yourself will affect your life, so will the beliefs you have about anything else. Make sure that your beliefs help you, not hinder you. Examine your core beliefs. Do they limit you? Do they set you up for continual disappointment? If so, recognize that and change them to beliefs that can empower you. For example, do you believe, "I'm too old?" Is that a good belief for you to have? Why not believe "Age means maturity and experience. I have a lot to offer!"? Get the picture?

What Do I Want?

"Thinking is the hardest work there is, which is the probable reason why so few engage in it."

— HENRY FORD

Now it is time to take stock of yourself and start the process of discovering just what your real values and beliefs are. To help you to do that, there are some exercises for you to do. Please do not just read through this section and think, "Oh, that's really interesting," and not do the exercises because that won't help you. Do these exercises as you come to them. Don't put it off. Don't think that you'll get back to this later. Procrastination is to be defeated at all costs! So, get a pen or pencil and lots of paper and go to a quiet place where you are comfortable, and arrange things so that you won't be interrupted by anyone (not even the telephone). Now it's time to start your journey into self-awareness. Remember, it is not going to be easy, it will take work, time, and stamina. Above all, you must be honest with yourself.

On a sheet of paper write down these sentences. Answer each as completely and as truthfully as you can.

The most important feelings to me in my life are:
The most important things to me in my life are:
I feel the most fulfilled in my life when I can:
I feel most satisfied in my life when I am:
What I want most in life is:

Once you have completed this exercise you will have a list of your values. Now identify the priority of your values. Think about which of your values are most important to you, and which are of lesser importance. Number them in terms of their significance to you. Their real significance — *not* what you think their importance *should* be. You will end up with your own hierarchy of values. Now for each value, write down the beliefs that you hold to be true for each value (like in the examples earlier). Notice if your beliefs are limiting or supportive. If some are confining you, write down a better alternative beside your old belief and cross out your old one.

This is not a simple exercise. It will take a great deal of thought and soul searching. Don't expect to complete this in five minutes. Take all the time you need. Don't rush yourself. This is too important. *Please do not read on until you have completed this exercise.*

You've finished. Okay. Let's go on. There are also negative values in your life. Values that make you feel awful. Things and emotions that you would do almost anything to avoid. Some examples of these values are:

pain	humiliation	dependence
anger	embarrassment	disappointment
betrayal	powerlessness	constriction
fear	failure	insecurity
deceit	depression	lack of control
defeat	frustration	loneliness

Now, on another sheet of paper write down these sentences and, again, answer them as completely and as truthfully as you can.

The feelings I hate the most in my life are:
The things I hate the most in my life are:
I feel the worst in my life when I:
I feel least satisfied in my life when I must:
What I want least in life is:

I am sure that you are feeling many of these emotions now. Which are the hardest for you to endure? As you did with your positive values, list your negative values and then number them in order of their importance to you, with number one being what you would do the most to avoid. Then outline the beliefs associated with each value. Are they keepers, or do you want to throw them out and replace them with new and better beliefs for you?

There. Whew. Take a breather if you want to. Not for too long.

You're back. Great. Just as you have positive and negative values in your life, you also have similar values in terms of your career. There are things about the industry you work in, the company you work for (or if you work for yourself), and the job you have that are important to look at. It is very important to know what your career values are because if you work in an environment or in a job that requires behaviour from you that either infringes on, contradicts, or even just doesn't support your own values you will experience inner conflict which will ultimately lead to unhappiness.

Corporations also have values. This is a company's corporate culture. The best scenario is when you can work in a company that has values congruent with your own. Then it will be less likely that you will find yourself experiencing inner turmoil over situations where you must violate one of your core values to reach an objective. If you are aware of your positive and negative values in your work, you will be able to find a job that meets and fulfills your values, instead of conflicting with them, and you will be in a comfortable environment that naturally suits you.

Time to take another sheet of paper out and answer these assertions as best you can.

The most important things to me in my career are:
I feel happiest in my job when I can:
I feel the most fulfilled in my job when I can:
I feel most satisfied in my job when I am:
The things that matter most to me in the industry I work for are:
The most important things to me in a company that I work for are:

Now to get at your negative career values, take out another sheet of paper and work on these statements.

The things I hated the most about my job were:
The least important things to me in my career are:
I felt worst in my job when I did:

I feel most unfulfilled in my career when I must:
What I want to avoid most in my career is:
The things I want to avoid in a company I work for are:

What do you value in the company and environment that you work in? To help you out, here are some things to think about:

- size of the company
- location of the company
- type of company (manufacturing, service, government, education)
- public versus private ownership
- motivation (profit, non-profit)
- ethics of the company (good corporate citizen?)
- bureaucratic versus responsive
- new versus established business
- hours of work (rigid versus flexible)
- surroundings (plush versus spartan)
- supportive of further education
- politics
- high pressure versus relaxed environment
- conformists versus individuality
- employee philosophy (work ethics)
- financial stability
- autonomous versus a division of a parent

What is most important to you in your job?

- money
- opportunity for advancement
- security
- profile
- your boss' management style
- social interaction (working on a team versus working alone)
- independence/freedom
- recognition

- structure
- responsibility
- challenge and growth versus repetition of tasks
- variety
- leadership
- office environment (shared or private)
- creativity
- travel

What would your ideal job be?
What would you be doing?
What company would be your ideal employer?
What industry most interests you?

Make sure that you examine the corporate culture and specifics of any potential company or job that you consider. Understand what the company values. See what the company rewards. Is there a match between your needs and that of the company and more specifically, the job? Make sure that your work style and values are consistent with that of the company and the job. It would be very unsettling if you worked for a company or in a job that forced you to be something that you are not.

Your values and beliefs will determine to a great extent how you will respond to all sorts of circumstances. Know what they are and don't put yourself in situations where you may have to behave in a manner that is inconsistent with your true self. Always be true to your values in life and in your career and you will lead a more happy, successful, and fulfilling life.

> *"The secret of happiness is not in doing what one likes, but in liking what one does."*
> — JAMES M. BARRIE

Skills And Strengths

Everyone has their own skills and strengths. The key is understanding your own unique set. This is not as easy as it sounds. You've got to dig deep to uncover and fully understand your natural abilities and aptitudes. Skills are things that you are proficient at. For example, you have work-related skills, which are things you were trained for or learned on the job. They are usually technical in nature, based on knowledge, and are things that your job title reflects. These types of skills are the easiest to identify. They are specific to your job or profession. Here are some examples:

managing/supervising	sales	legal tenders
bookkeeping	marketing	purchasing
financial planning	contracts	budgeting
designing software	design	product development
international relations	writing	policy formulation

Write down all the work-related skills that you have. I'm sure that it will be quite a long list. When you think that your list is complete, think again. I'm sure that there are a few that you forgot. Now, from amongst this group of skills, you will have particular strengths in some of these areas. For example, you may be a skilled financial analyst, but your strength is in reading financial statements and identifying potential problems or opportunities. Or you may be a marketing professional, with an expertise in conceptualizing new, exciting promotions. Skills are things that you do well, whereas, strengths are the things that you do exceptionally well and enjoy doing. Write down what your strengths are.

Another set of skills you have are personal skills. They define your personality and are shaped by your attitudes. They are demonstrated on the job in terms of your work style and are also part of everything that you do. Some examples of personal skills are:

flexibility	judgement	assertiveness
persistence	leadership	patience
initiative	sensitivity	stability
resourcefulness	organization	attentiveness
co-operation	reliability	discipline
consideration	diplomacy	charisma

Are you a good negotiator? Persuader? Communicator? Problem solver? Analyst? Conflict resolver? Are you good with people?

These are all personal skills. What else do you do well? What do you excel at? What do you enjoy doing? Write down all these skills and strengths.

Some of these abilities may be so ingrained in you and may come so naturally that they may be very difficult to isolate and identify as specific aptitudes. Here are some exercises to help you.

Examine *all* of your life experiences (school, work, hobbies, leisure, volunteer). Then make a list of all the times you felt happiest. Include all of the things you enjoyed doing most. Write down all your successes and accomplishments. Which ones made you feel the greatest? Which experiences made you feel most proud? Go as far back into your past as you can. Anything that you did that made you feel really good should be on this list.

Have you done your list? If not please go back and complete it. You've done your list? Okay. On to the next step.

For each item on this list, break down the experience to examine the components of the situation. Why did you feel great? What was it about that experience that made you feel wonderful? What skills did you use in each case? Be honest. Be objective. Keep digging. Look for items and words that keep coming up. These are your core skills and strengths. These are the aptitudes and attributes you have that make you feel good when you use them.

For example, you may have felt absolutely great when you completed a very complex model. What were the skills involved in doing that?

dexterity	patience	creativity
analysis	mastery	attention to detail
design	closure	foresight

Or, you might have felt incredibly proud when you graduated with your law degree. What skills did completing law school take?

intelligence	learning	discipline
persistence	diligence	problem-solving
study	memory	communication

Or, you may have felt on top of the world when you taught your son to ride a bicycle. What skills did you pull out of your bag for that?

| patience | teaching | helping |
| communication | persistence | leadership |

Or, you may have felt fabulous when your client finally agreed to your proposal. What were the skills that you used?

negotiation	selling	analyzing
communication	intelligence	reading people
problem-solving	deal-making	persuasion

Be relentless. You must keep at it. This is not an easy process. You do not have to do this exercise in one sitting. This may take you days to do properly. Discipline yourself. Stretch yourself. Push yourself. It will be worth it.

Now, on another sheet of paper, write down all the things that you do not like to do, either in the work place or in your personal life. What things frustrate you? What do you need to improve at? Where do your weaknesses lie? Examine all of your life experiences. Look at things that you have done or situations you were in that you felt the most unhappy, that you least enjoyed, and that you felt the most frustrated and dissatisfied with. Figure out why you felt that way. Then isolate the areas that you are weakest in or dislike the most. Then you'll know what to avoid. You will also know the things that you need to improve at. It is really important here (and hardest) to be objective and honest with yourself.

"Only the curious will learn and only the resolute will overcome the obstacles to learning."

— Eugine S. Wilson

Talents, Interests, And Passions

"A musician must make music, an artist must paint, a poet must write, if he is to be ultimately at peace with himself."
— ABRAHAM MASLOW

The greatest job fulfillment you can get is if you have a special talent (and we all do), interest, or a passion and you can incorporate that in your job. Musicians, actors, and artists are the most obvious examples of that.

However, there are all sorts of talents. The first step is identifying them. You may have a real talent for motivating people, or building a business, or spotting trends. You may be very creative and not even know it. Whatever your talent, if you are not using it, you are wasting one of your greatest natural assets. You will also probably not feel totally fulfilled. For example, if you are great at start-ups of new ventures, you would probably not be happy working at or even running a stable ongoing business. You may be very creative and have a real talent for writing, however you may not even be aware of it if you have never had the opportunity to use that gift in your previous jobs.

You may have a hobby that you are very interested in and excited about. If you could include that as part of your job, you would be on the yellow brick road. For example, if you've always had a green thumb and loved tending your garden, you may want to think about a career in horticulture. Or, if you love sports and you worked in a sports-event management company, you would be excited about going into work every day. Not only that, but you would be passionate about your work, which would make you energized and motivated. You couldn't help but be happy and successful at your job. You'd be getting paid to do what you love! Search for your talents and your passions. Discover and be true to your real self. Success will then come naturally.

Karen L.'s story is a good example of how important it is to know yourself and be able to recognize a match between yourself and the company you work for. It also exemplifies the desirability of incorporating your interests into your job.

"I had been working for years at different jobs. I always quit after a relatively short period of time because I never felt happy or comfortable in any job. I always felt dissatisfied and left. (That pattern was not helping me to build a career!) After I quit my job at a financial institution, I again wondered what I wanted to do. I decided to sign up with a temporary employment agency and try my hand at many different things. One of my temporary assignments was at a large packaging firm. My job was in the accounting department. I worked there with one other fellow. He was a real company guy. He organized sports pools, made sure there was always beer at the company's parties and other activities, and would often go out after work for a drink with people from the office. He was everybody's buddy. The funny thing is, though, that he couldn't do his job well. He cost the company money in overtime and mistakes. When I came in, I was so efficient at getting the job done that the company extended my contract. Then after six months I was fired.

"I couldn't believe it! I was fired because I didn't fit in. Even though I knew that the job was a temporary position and it was not what I wanted to do with the rest of my life, that did not stop me from feeling devastated. I had to spend that week in bed! All I could think of was, 'How could I be fired?' and 'How dare they?!' It is such a shock to be fired, but I think that it was a very valuable experience for me because I learned a lot about myself.

"Being fired forced me to really examine myself and how the business world works. I realized that companies would rather have an inefficient worker that fit in really well, than someone who did a really good job, who did not fit in. I also realized why I had never been happy in all my previous jobs. There are certain systems and environments that just don't match me and therefore lead to discontent. That realization changed my life. I sat down and thought a lot about who I was, what I needed and wanted in a job and in a work environment, what I had to offer, what I would enjoy doing, and where I would fit in. Then, based on this new knowledge and insight I made a list of companies that I wanted to work for. Instead of looking in the want ads, I targeted companies and jobs that I felt were best suited for me.

"That process led me to joining a television station, where I've been happily working for six years. I targeted that company in my mind, and it's funny, things just started to happen. There were two job opportunities at the television station, both of which I applied for and both of which I got turned down for. But I kept persisting (knowing that I really wanted to work for that station), and on my third try I got hired! I truly love my job. I make good money and I have a great deal of responsibility, but best of all, I really fit in at the station.

"I know that if I hadn't gotten fired, I would not have been forced to really evaluate what went wrong and why. I would have kept making the same mistakes, working at the same type of companies, never enjoying what I was doing, and never getting anywhere. Being fired threw me out of that endless, self-defeating, working loop into positive self-analysis and for that I am thankful. The sad thing is, many people don't enjoy their jobs and never bother to understand why, or try to make their lives better. I'm very lucky now. I am in charge of all the entertainment at the television station, so I deal with things that I love in my own personal life. I am very grateful that I can incorporate my pleasures and interests into my work.

"Being fired is extremely painful when it happens. However, it is interesting how most painful experiences have a lesson in them. For me, being fired was a very valuable tool. I learned a great deal from it, and if it did not happen I would certainly not be where I am today."

Enough with that heavy stuff. Now it is time to dream, fantasize, and imagine. What would you do if you knew you couldn't fail? What would you do if you won a lottery worth a couple of million dollars? What is your career fantasy? Compare your answers with the results of the other exercises. See a pattern?

Now it is time for a reality check. Call up people who know you well, or who have worked with you, and ask them what they think you do best. Ask them where they think your skills and talents lie. Ask each person you call to tell you the top three things that they think you excel at. Then break that down into skill components and compare that to your findings. See any similarities?

You should now know who you are, what you want, and where you want to be. You have set your priorities and you have a clear understanding of what is important to you. You are familiar with your skills, strengths, capabilities, and accomplishments. Now you can direct your job search to the types of jobs and companies that you are best suited for. You can target and focus your search. (You will be more likely to make a correct hit if you are focusing on a clear target.) You can use this self-knowledge and insight to package yourself to the right companies and more effectively sell yourself to the companies you choose to target. Not only will you feel more comfortable with yourself, but you will be better able to answer questions during your job interviews in a concise, credible, and direct manner. You won't be scrambling when an interviewer asks you, "So, tell me about yourself." (Make sure that you answer that question in a way that is relevant to the job.) Remember, the better you know yourself, the better you can positively communicate about yourself in a relevant way, and therefore the more likely it is that you will get the right job.

If you had trouble working through these self-analysis exercises there are career counselling services that can help you in this process. Some places to look for help are:

- community colleges
- local school boards
- local YMCA
- the Yellow Pages under Career Counselling

Talk to a few places. Meet the counsellor you would be working with. It is important that you feel comfortable with that person because you will have to share very personal experiences and feelings with your counsellor. Also shop around. Find out what the cost is. Find out if you have to buy a package or if you can buy components. Know what your needs are and what your options are.

A Quick Review

Do you know and can you identify:

- your values — in life and work.
- your beliefs — do they support you.
- your skills, style, talents, strengths, weaknesses.
- your interests, hobbies, passions.
- your accomplishments, successes.
- how others see you.
- how to communicate your aptitudes with relevance to the job at hand.

If you get focused, work hard, and stay true to yourself, you will be successful in your job search, but more than that you will be motivated, fulfilled, and happy at your next job. Believe in and respect yourself. Don't try to be who you are not. You've got untapped potential within you just waiting to be explored! Be adventurous! Discover what is special and unique about you. Don't impose limits on yourself. You can make your dreams come true. The secret is within you.

Now that you know who you are and what you want, you need to know how to achieve it. You need a plan of action.

> *"The greatest end in life is not knowledge but action."*
>
> — Thomas Henry Huxley

How Do I Get There From Here?

"Obstacles are those frightful things you see when you take your eyes off your goals."

— Anonymous

You need a road map to help you navigate along your path to your destination — happiness — which of course includes job satisfaction. Before you can design your map, you need to know clearly where you are, what you want, what you will need to do to get it, and how you will achieve your objectives. You now know all about yourself, where you are in your life and career, and what you would like to do in your next job. Let's take that a step further.

You need to have short- and long-term goals for your life and your career. Goal-setting is very, very important because you need to be able to know and articulate what you want before you can get it. You can design things in your life the way you want them to be. *You* are in control. How do you do this? The first step is to define your goals. Setting goals allows you to focus your attention on what you want, and as you saw in Chapter 3, what you focus on you tend to get.

Goals should be:

- written down — that makes it more concrete and real.

- directed at what you want; not what you do not want. For example, "I want to lose fifty pounds" versus "I don't want to be fat."

- as specific as possible — the more detailed you can be, the better.

- just outside your grasp, but not out of your sight.

Your goals should also have a target date for achievement and milestones of success along the way.

Armed with your self-knowledge, make a list of your top ten short-term goals — that is, what would you like to accomplish within this year? These goals should include career, financial, and personal items. Write them down. The power of written goals cannot be underestimated. Don't forget to include your deadline for the achievement of each goal. Here is an example of a short-term goal list:

1. Get hired at the right job for me in the next three months. (And now you know what that is so be specific here.) I want to get a job as a project manager in the environmental industry in a mid-sized, entrepreneurial-style company in the not-for-profit sector of the economy.

2. Make $100,000 by year-end.

3. Quit smoking by October.

4. Lose twenty pounds by June.

5. Take my family on a vacation for one week to Disneyland this year.

6. Exercise three times a week regularly starting today.

7. Take a computer course at a community college enrolling this fall.

8. Paint the garage this summer.

9. Work on my tennis game and be able to beat Frank by August.

10. Visit my parents at least once a month starting this month.

Now, think of why you want to achieve each of these goals. Why are they important to you? Which ones are most important to you? Why? Write down your reasons. Now look at your top five goals. What do you need to do to achieve them? What steps do you have to take from where you are now to attain these goals? What actions can you take *today* to bring you closer to reaching your goals? In answering these questions, you will make an *Action Plan*. Commit yourself to the achievement of these goals.

Believe you will attain them. But remember: *thoughts and intentions without action will get you* **nowhere!**

You need to take action in accordance with your plan. You can now have a set of objectives for each day, for each week, and for each month. These objectives will be the milestones and benchmarks in your quest to achieve your goals. As you successfully pass each benchmark, reward yourself. Recognize and appreciate what you achieved each day, each week, and each month. Then when you reach your goals, you can really celebrate (you will deserve it). Then it will be time to plan your next steps. Don't forget to take pride in all your victories, large or small. Enjoy the journey, not just the destination.

> *"Live your life each day as you would climb a mountain. An occasional glance toward the summit keeps the goal in mind, but so many beautiful scenes are to be observed from each new vantage point. Climb slowly, steadily, enjoying each passing moment; and the view from the summit will serve as a fitting climax for the journey."*
>
> — HAROLD V. MELCHERT

Make sure that you review your goals often. If after writing them down, you put the list in a drawer and don't look at it again it will do you little good. Monitor your progress. As you finish each day, check off all the objectives that you reached. That will give you a great sense of accomplishment, which will in turn boost your confidence and your self-esteem.

Now it is time to look at your long-range goals. You need to have a plan for your life. Make a list of what you would like to achieve in the next five to ten years. Again, make sure each goal has a target date and is as specific as possible.

- Do you want to pay off your mortgage? By when?
- Do you want to own your own business? What type of business? By when?

- Do you want to be president of a large company? What kind of company? By when?

- Do you want to write a novel? About what? By when?

- Do you want to buy a new house? Where? What kind? By when?

- Do you want to learn another language? Which one? By when?

- What are your financial goals?

- What are your career goals?

- What are your personal goals?

- If you were very old, would you look back on your life and wish that you had done something? What?

Now you have a list of your long-term goals. Make sure that your short-term goals support your long-term goals. For each goal write down why it is important to you. Write down as many compelling reasons that you can think of. This will help you motivate yourself to achieve your goals. What do you need to do to reach your goals? What can you do today? This week? This year? Make an action plan, and commit yourself to following it with the caveat that things change and people change. Review your goals on a regular basis. See if your goals are limiting you. Do they still work for you? Are they encouraging you to stretch yourself? Do you need to change your approach? Should some goals be discarded and replaced with more empowering ones? Do some deadlines need to be revised? (You may even reach some goals before your target dates!) The key is to review your goals often and on a regular basis. Monitor your progress and the suitability of your goals.

Don't lose sight of what you want and go after it!

You CAN get there from here. You now have your road map and you are in the driver's seat. Keep in mind that it won't be easy. There will always be bumps in the road and unexpected detours. But you will arrive at your

destination if you keep sight of your goals, keep travelling
in the right direction, and along the right road.
Bon Voyage!

> *"Far away there in the sunshine are my high-*
> *est aspirations. I may not reach them, but I*
> *can look up and see their beauty, believe in*
> *them and try to follow where they lead."*
>
> — LOUISA MAY ALCOTT

CHAPTER 5...

Where Do I Go From Here?

The Job Search Process

*"Happiness lies in the joy of achievement and
the thrill of creative effort."*
—FRANKLIN ROOSEVELT

Looking for a job is a job. In fact, it is probably the hardest job you'll ever have. At least in your last position, you were qualified for what you were doing and you knew how to do your job. Now you are faced with a full-time job that you are unprepared for. You may not have had to look for a job in *years*. In fact, you may *never* have had to go through the job search process. You may have been recruited out of school and stayed at the same company working your way up; or you may have had other jobs come to you.

Whatever the case may be, looking for a job in the nineties is a demanding, tough, frustrating, lonely, and challenging process. There is a great deal of competition out there in the job hunting market. In order to be successful in your pursuit for the right job, you must be creative, persistent, resilient, focused, positive, prepared, energetic, assertive, and enthusiastic.

Yet, your ego will be tested and re-tested, you will feel like giving up at times, and you may go through weeks of "thanks, but no thanks" letters and unreturned phone calls. The key is not to take any of this personally. It is not a rejection of you. It is just circumstance.

You will feel discouraged and miserable at times. Don't let that overcome you. If you feel that you are getting nowhere, or starting to feel depressed, take a break. Do something nice for yourself. Know when you are approaching your limit, and stop for awhile. Even in your old jobs you had sick days and vacations. When you feel you need an hour or a day off —take it — and *don't feel guilty* about it. If you are working hard at your job search, you deserve a break once in a while. Enjoy it. But do not break for too long. Don't lose your rhythm. Keep at it. Use your prime time (8:30 a.m. to 5:30 p.m.) wisely. Renovations on the house and other large time-consuming projects should be saved for the weekends.

As suggested in Chapter 1, if you don't have the services of an outplacement facility to conduct your job search from, set aside a part of your house or apartment as your "office." Establish a routine for yourself and stick to it. Try to include some enjoyable or relaxing things, and physical exercise in your daily schedule to reduce the impact of the stress of the job search process. You may want to take a part-time job or do volunteer work. As mentioned earlier in this book, volunteer work will get you out meeting people and contributing and you will feel better about yourself. Or you may want to improve yourself, take a course, read, listen to motivational tapes, or learn a skill that you never had the time to learn. It is important to use your time productively. Keep up your physical health and your appearance. Dress in your business attire every day and you will feel more resourceful.

Your attitude is the fuel that powers your job search. It will keep you going, or make you sputter out. So, try to keep a positive attitude. Reward yourself for small successes. Don't give up. Keep believing in yourself. Some days this will be harder to do than others, but, if overall you don't believe in yourself how can you convince an interviewer to believe in you? Remember, it is not always the most qualified candidate that gets the job; it is the person who can best *convince* the interviewers that he or she is the best person for the job! Expect to succeed and you eventually will.

Now, because knowing how to get a job is as important as knowing how to do a job, let's examine the components of a successful job search. But remember, expect rejection and don't take it to heart. You won't get every job you go after, but you will ultimately get the right job for you. The key to a successful job search is persistence. Keep trying and don't let the search process get you down. You will have some bad days, but on the whole, try to stay up on yourself and enthusiastic. Be determined and focused and you will ultimately be successful in your job search.

"The worst bankrupt person in the world is the person who has lost his enthusiasm."
—H.W Arnold

Outplacement Services

Outplacement, relocation or re-employment companies, services, consultants or counsellors are the terms used to describe the business of helping ousted employees cope with job loss and assist them in finding a new position. They will not get you a job; you have to do that yourself. But they will teach you and guide you through the job search process. (For the purposes of simplicity in this book, outplacement is the term that is used.)

Most dismissals are not directly the fault of the employee or a result of "just cause." Ties are usually cut due to personality conflicts, economics, or changes in company ownership or philosophy. Therefore, when escorting management out the door, companies want to ease the pain of the exiting employee and relieve the guilt of the firing employer (and reduce the chances of a lawsuit). They do this by utilizing the services of professional outplacement firms. The outplacement services are usually paid for by the ex-employee's company as part of a severance package. Some outplacement companies (not all of them) do allow dismissed executives to purchase their services; but, keep in mind that this can be very expensive expertise. Therefore, if the services of an outplacement firm is a part of your severance package, you are lucky. If it was not a part of your severance package, you may want to consider asking for it. As mentioned in Chapter 1, these firms are not a pipe line back to your old company. It is a service for you.

Usually you will be introduced to your outplacement counsellor immediately following the termination meeting. If it is left up to you to contact the counsellor, do so right away. These professional consultants will help you to diffuse your resentment, re-build your shaken confidence and shattered ego, and focus your energies on thinking and acting positively to find your next rewarding job and a better future.

An executive without a job is like a fish out of water. You will be floundering. You may not know where to turn to or what to do. You may be unprepared for the rigors of a long, tough job search. Outplacement firms will provide you with a structure and a strategy for your search. They will help you to cope with your loss, will inform you about the job search process, and will coach you along the way. They are professionals and their expertise is valuable. Use it.

There are different types and levels of packages offered by outplacement companies. All of them will give you an "office" to conduct your search from (some may be private; others may have to be shared), complete with secretarial services to type and send out your correspondence and take messages for you. Some other services offered by outplacement firms are:

- counselling (moral and practical support to help you adjust to and cope with job loss).

- assistance in dealing with family and friends.

- financial counselling.

- personal and career assessment.

- job search strategies and techniques (identification of appropriate targets and a strategy for penetrating target industries, companies, and jobs).

- information and advice on self-employment issues.

- preparation of résumés and letters.

- advice on how to deal with references.

- interview preparation and training.

- advice on how to evaluate job offers.

Make sure that you know what your package entails. Also, most outplacement contracts have a fixed term. They usually last for six months to one year. Occasionally your company may give you the service until you find re-employment; but this is rare these days. Outplacement firms are a valuable source of information, guidance, and support. But remember, outplacement firms will not get you a job. They will help you and provide you with the right tools, but only *you* can get you a job.

The Résumé

Your résumé is your most important job search tool. It is your sales brochure and must showcase you in your best possible light. The purpose of a résumé is to get potential employers interested enough in you to grant you an interview. It is a door-opener. It must grab the attention of the person screening the résumés. Often, (especially in tough economic times) a company may receive 500 résumés for one job opening! Therefore, the screeners do not have the time to carefully read each résumé thoroughly. You must attract the reader in the first one and a half minutes! You have to sell yourself on the first page. You need to communicate who you are and what you have to offer up front. It is not always the best candidates who get the interviews, but the ones who look the best on paper, that is, the ones with the most effective résumés.

Remember the story on Harry P. from Chapter 3? He sent out over 450 résumés to no avail. It wasn't until he got other people's opinions of his résumé and their helpful advice as to how to change it to make it more effective, that he finally started to generate positive responses. Neither he nor his experience were different, the only thing that he changed was how he communicated that information on his résumé. And talk about persistence! He never gave up. He sent out over 500 résumés before he got his job. If he had not persevered and kept at it, he would not have found the job he currently is enjoying. And according to Peter, the right job was worth the effort.

Let's examine:

- What makes a great résumé.
- What employers look for in a résumé.

People who screen résumés are human (although sometimes you will wonder if that is really true!). They are individuals and they have their own preferences, biases, and practices. However, there are some general guidelines to follow when writing your résumé. Please take care in putting together your résumé. It can mean the difference between success in generating interviews or failure time and time again. Résumé preparation will take time, effort, and re-draft after re-draft. Then, when you feel satisfied, have someone that you respect (and who has good attention to detail) check it over for grammar, spelling, and overall look and feel. You will probably have to change it again. Keep at it until you have a great sales piece that reflects the best impression of you. Don't send out a résumé that isn't your best effort.

Here are some résumé preparation tips:

- Your résumé must be typed, neat, brief, concise, and easy-to-read. It must have an eye-appealing layout and your most important features should be easily noticed. It should not exceed two pages.
- Your résumé should be accomplishment oriented. It is not a job description. Quantify your accomplishments wherever possible. Use action words. To help you there is a list of action words in the Appendix at the end of this chapter. (The list is by no means exhaustive, but it will serve to stimulate your thinking.)
- Put your personal information on top:
  Name
  Address
  Phone Number
  Education: school attended, degree, date of graduation *if appropriate* — if you are a recent graduate or

you have a degree of distinction (M.B.A., C.A. L.L.B. etc.). If this is not the case, then list your education at the end of your work history. *Do not* include your age, place of birth, sex, health, race, marital status, political or religious affiliation.

- Do mention any languages that you are fluent in.

- Include your hobbies, volunteer work, professional memberships briefly at the bottom of your résumé.

- At the end of your résumé state that references will be available upon request. It is not necessary to attach that list to your résumé.

- Use bullet points (there is no need for lengthy prose).

- Your résumé must be well organized and have *no* spelling or grammatical mistakes.

- Copy your résumé on good quality 8 1/2 by 11 inch white or light-coloured (beige or grey) paper. Stay away from legal-size paper and bright-coloured (orange, blue, red, pink, or green) paper. Unless you are in a very creative industry it is best to avoid gimmicks and be conservative.

- Make sure you have good quality, clean copies of your résumé.The best bet is to go to your local print shop and have them make you copies. Ask for a quantity discount. Print shops also have a wide variety of paper stocks to choose from.

- Title your résumé with either your name or simply "Résumé."

- Think twice before you include a career objective. If it is too specific, it can limit you, and if it is too general it is meaningless. You may want to have a few versions of your résumé with differing career objectives on them to target different career alternatives. There are different schools of thought concerning putting career objectives on a résumé. It is your personal choice.

- Don't mention salary.
- Don't send a photograph.
- Don't give reasons for leaving your last job.
- Don't use jargon or slang.
- Don't include confidential information about any of your former employers.

There are two generally accepted résumé formats: one is chronoligical, one is functional.

1. **The Chronological Résumé:** This is the most used, accepted, understood, and preferred format. It lists your work experience in reverse chronological order dating back to your first job out of school. Your career profile should follow your personal information and should include dates of employment, name (and sometimes the type) of company, your position, and a concise outline of your major responsibilities and accomplishments. As you go back in time, fewer details are necessary. (Potential employers may find what you did twenty years ago irrelevant to their current needs!) Try to show growth and progression in your career. If appropriate, mention transfers and promotions within the same company. Your hobbies, volunteer work, professional memberships, and languages spoken should follow your work history. There is an example of a chronological résumé in the Appendix at the end of this chapter.

2. **The Functional Résumé:** This format is organized by skills and abilities, as opposed to specific jobs and companies. Instead of company name, date and title headings, you group experiences under areas of expertise and functional skills that are transferable between jobs. This format is advisable when you

want to make a career change or you have changed jobs often.(On average, an employer may think you are a job hopper if you have changed jobs more than once every two or three years.) For this type of résumé you should still include a brief list of your employers (with or without dates as is appropriate) after your functional accomplishments because potential employers do want to know where you got your experience. It also adds credibility to your résumé. There is an example of a functional résumé in the Appendix at the end of this chapter.

Make sure that your résumé, whether it is chronological or functional, focuses on your accomplishments and your successes. Remember, your résumé should reflect the best possible you. If you are getting the assistance of an outplacement firm in résumé writing, make sure it is not too slick. Recruiters can spot assembly-line résumés which make it difficult for the reader to get a feel for the real person. So, follow the guidelines suggested by your outplacement counsellor, but make sure you add your own personal touch to your résumé. Take your time and prepare the best résumé you can. Don't be screened out! Let your résumé work for you not against you. If you need further help in preparing your résumé, you can find assistance at community colleges, career counselling centres, your local YMCA, and at the library. There are also many books that have been written on résumé writing.

The Covering Letter

No résumé should ever be sent out without a covering letter attached to it. The letter should be no more than one page, and should be typewritten on the same stock as your résumé. Similar to your résumé, the covering letter should be concise, free of grammatical and spelling errors, and pleasing to the eye. (Short paragraphs work best.) Unlike your résumé, the covering letter should be custom-tailored to each job opportunity, company, or person it is sent to. Make sure that you properly spell both the company name and the person's name that you are addressing the letter to. Also, ensure that you have the correct job title. Directories quickly become outdated, so a quick telephone call to the company switchboard to check on these items is well worth the effort.

Your covering letter allows you to highlight certain issues or accomplishments and allows more of your personality to come through. Covering letters serve as the preface to your résumé. They should catch a person's interest and answer the question: "Why should I read this letter?" There are many ways to hook a reader's attention. For example:

- If you are responding to an advertisement, say so up front (preferably in your first sentence). Briefly show how your skills and experience match those that are required for the job. Make sure that you have read the advertisement carefully and have picked out the qualities and skills that they listed as necessary for the position.

- Name drop, that is, mention that a mutual friend has recommended that you write to this person. (Of course this has to be true!)

- Address a problem the industry or company is facing.

- Congratulate the person you are writing to on their recent promotion or successful deal.

- Comment on a speech you heard that person make, or a remark that person made in the media.

- Say that you want to further develop a certain skill and their company would be the best place to do so and then state why.

Once you've got the reader's attention in the first paragraph, the second and third paragraphs should highlight who you are, what you can do for them, and why you want to work for that company or person. Briefly highlight some relevant accomplishments and give the reader a reason to want to meet with you. The final paragraph should directly ask for an interview and propose a follow-up schedule.

Remember, the covering letter is your first impression. It is your introduction to the potential employer. Don't blow it. Here are some things to remember:

- Your letter must have a positive tone to it.

- Be brief and direct.

- Always ask for a meeting; propose a follow-up schedule and stick to it. For example, if you say in your letter that you will contact that person on a particular day or in a particular time frame — do it! Don't be late or lazy with your follow up.

- Address letters to individuals in the company, not to the faceless Human Resources department or the invisible Sir or Madam.

- Mark the envelope personal and confidential.

- The envelope should match the paper stock that your covering letter and résumé are printed on.

- Always date the letter and then mail it on the same day.

- Let some of your personality come through. Differentiate yourself.

- Include your phone number under your name in case the letter becomes separated from the résumé.

- Avoid the appearance of mass mailing. Individualize each letter.

- Don't forget to sign your name! You would not be the first person to forget!

There is an example of a covering letter in the Appendix at the end of this chapter.

You may also want to send your covering letter and résumé by fax. If you do, remember that fax machines are not private and the quality that comes out is not the best. If you do send your résumé by fax, follow it up with the original by mail and call to make sure that the letter and résumé were received.

The Job Search

Research

After you have targeted industries and companies that you want to work in, you must do your homework. Make sure you research those industries and companies. Find out what major issues, problems, opportunities, and trends are facing the industry and the company. (For example, how has free trade had an impact on the way they do business.) Know the company's concerns, products, and plans. Be able to write an informed, intelligent letter and be able to converse with potential employers in their language. Be aware of their needs. Then you can set yourself up as a bright, knowledgeable problem-solver.

You can gather a great deal of information at your local library. You can access trade directories and publications, business journals, and the annual reports of public companies. Also, stay informed about current business affairs reported in the media. Have a good feel and general knowledge of the industries and companies that you want to target. Then, when you get an interview with one of your target companies, you should research it more in depth. (We will look further into research for interview preparation in the section on interviewing.)

The Job Market

There are two parts to the job market: the visible job market and the hidden job market.

1. **The Visible Job Market:** There is the visible job market, which incorporates all publicly known jobs.

To search in this market, you must read the newspapers and trade magazines and reply to job advertisements that apply to you. It is very difficult to get a job this way, because the competition is fierce. For every advertised position, an employer can receive up to 500 applications (or even more)! The odds are not in your favour. This doesn't mean that it can't happen though, so don't give up trying.

Another source for the visible job market is placement through executive search firms, executive recruiters, employment or placement agencies or, as they are commonly referred to, headhunters. These firms know of job openings and try to fill them with the right candidates. Either way, the job opening is known about and there is heavy competition to fill each position.

2. **The Hidden Job Market:** The other part of the job market is called the hidden job market. This is where you find a job before it is made public, or create your own opportunity. The hidden job market is tapped through broadcast letters, networking, and advice or information-gathering meetings. It is estimated that over 80% of middle- to senior-level positions are found through the hidden job market.

Let's look more closely at each element of your job search campaign.

Job Search Techniques
The Visible Job Market
Responding To Advertisements

The most obvious way to look for a job, and one you can't ignore, is to search the classified and career sections of the daily newspapers — *every day*. Also, look at industry magazines and papers. They usually carry job opportunities at the back of each publication. Each ad will tell you what the job requires and what skills, abilities, and experience the employer is seeking. Examine each ad and underline or highlight the key words and requirements. Then, when you write your covering letter be sure to:

- Say in your first sentence that you are writing in response to their advertisement (it is helpful if you can mention the publication and date of the ad).

- Emphasize how your skills, abilities, experience, and background fit with those key requirements mentioned in the ad. Respond directly to the duties and qualifications in the ad using the actual words that were used in the advertisement.

- Ask for an interview directly and positively.

- Send off the covering letter with your résumé as soon after the ad runs as possible.

Keep copies of all of the letters that you send out and staple each ad to each corresponding letter and file it for follow up. This will also help if you are called, you can quickly pull out the ad and refer to the qualifications required during your telephone conversation. If you are not called, make sure you make a follow-up call approximately five working days after you sent out your letter and résumé. Again, ask for an interview politely and positively. Don't expect to get a response from every approach, and you will be less disappointed. But be persistent and don't give up. An example of an advertisement and corresponding covering letter is in the Appendix at the end of this chapter.

EXECUTIVE SEARCH CONSULTANTS (HEADHUNTERS)

These agencies place people in positions that are available. Find out which are the firms that specialize in your field. If you do not know which are the top firms in your industry (or the industry you want to enter), talk to colleagues or senior people in that industry and ask for a recommendation. They will tell you which firms are respectable and which firms to stay away from. Some agencies are better to deal with than others. (For example, avoid agencies that irritate employers by their aggressive tactics.) Then select two or three of these key firms that you feel will represent you best and meet and register with them. Don't become involved with too many firms, as that will devalue your worth and there will be no incentive for any executive search firm to work hard for you.

Many of these firms can be helpful to you if you know how to work effectively with them. The relationship between you and a search consultant is a mutually beneficial business relationship. You do not go there looking for sympathy or pity, and you don't approach them with a "so what can you do for me" attitude. Realize that you are not the client. The company who is hiring is the client. The recruiter is paid to find the best candidate for the job. Sometimes they are on retainer and get paid regardless of whether they fill the position; others are paid a percentage of the successful candidate's salary and therefore only get paid if they fill the position. It is in your best interest to work with executive recruiters and form an alliance with them. Respond to their needs. Convince them that you are the best candidate. You want the recruiter to believe in your abilities and your suitability for positions so that they will convince the hiring client that you should get the job. But don't sit back and rely on these search firms to get you a job. You've also got to delve into the hidden job market.

> *"Don't wait for your ship to come in. Swim out to it."*
>
> —Unknown

The Hidden Job Market

It is more beneficial to spend the majority of your job search time penetrating the hidden job market as opposed to answering ads and massaging executive search companies, because your chances of success are much higher.

Here are some tools you can use to infiltrate the hidden job market:

BROADCAST LETTERS

The broadcast letter is similar in many ways to the covering letter. The objective of the broadcast letter is to get an interview. It is like a sales cold call. It is not written in response to an opening, but it tries to get your foot in the door and makes you known to a person who could be in a position to hire you. The letter should be no longer than one page (typewritten) and on good quality paper stock. It should have short paragraphs and a pleasing layout. The broadcast letter should be addressed to a specific person (ideally two levels above your own). Never send this type of letter to the Human Resources department or a personnel manager. The key is to make direct contact with a person who can hire you now or in the future. Make sure that the person's name is spelled correctly and the title is accurate. It should be letter-perfect, clear, and concise. The broadcast letter should end with a request for an interview and a suggestion for follow-up steps. It should not mention salary or references.

This is where the similarities between a broadcast letter and a covering letter end. The main difference between these two types of letters is that the broadcast letter is *not* accompanied by your résumé. It goes solo. This is a particularly effective tool if you are changing industries, have changed jobs frequently, or if you have limited experience, because you can emphasize only the parts of your experience that are relevant to the job you are seeking without having to disclose all the details of your work history. It lets you highlight what you have to offer a particular employer without the distraction of the non-applicable (and perhaps negative) details of your résumé. The broadcast letter is an effective way of emphasizing your achievements and your experiences that apply directly to the reader's industry, and, therefore, address your reader's needs head on.

Catch the reader's interest up front. Make sure when you read all the newspapers and trade magazines that you not only read the classifieds, but you read the entire paper and look for opportunities. Read between the lines. Watch television and listen to the radio for news and business interest items. There are many stories that can serve as a lead in to your letters. Also, don't forget to include your address and phone number on the broadcast letters! And who knows, you may have uncovered a job opportunity! These letters are sent out cold, so don't expect an overwhelming response. Be sure to follow up by telephone and again ask for an interview. By the way, don't forget to conduct your search in a focused manner. Twenty well-targeted letters are much more effective than fifty unfocused letters. An example of a broadcast letter is included in the Appendix at the end of this chapter.

NETWORKING

It is estimated that most of management and senior level jobs are obtained through networking. Your personal contacts are your best source for job leads. This is especially true in tough economic times or when competition is high. Telling people that you are in the job market and asking for their help and advice is not begging or belittling. It is advertising yourself. There is no shame or embarrassment in getting the word out that you are available for work. In fact, most of your contacts will be happy to help you. Of course, they will require direction from you. Call them up and ask for their help in a direct and specific manner. Tell them your goals and ask if they can help you in pursuing your objectives, or if they know anyone who could. You may want to meet with them and talk to them face to face. Try to get at least two other names of people to call from each person you speak to, even if they can't help you directly. Then your network will grow and grow. Networking is a numbers game. The wider you cast your net, the more likely it is that you will catch the fish!

Networking is the best way to tap into the hidden job market. Start by making a list of people you can call. Who are your contacts? Basically, anyone who knows (and likes) you is a contact. For example:

- former employers, subordinates, colleagues, clients, suppliers
- friends, relatives, neighbours, and acquaintances
- friends and acquaintances of your spouse or close friends
- parents of your children's friends
- your accountant, lawyer, banker, insurance agent
- old schoolmates
- members of your country club, trade association, gym

Tell them your situation and what you want and how they can help you. Make sure they are familiar with your background and your career objectives. In fact, you may want to send a few key contacts your résumé. Ask for their opinion. You may get some good free advice, and they will have it handy to refer to when talking about you to their contacts! Keep a record of all your calls, meetings, and referrals. When a contact refers you to someone, call that person right away and make sure to mention your sponsor's name. For example, you may want to say something like: "A mutual friend of ours, John Smith, recommended that I call you. I am . . . looking for . . . and I can offer. . . ." Then try to get a meeting with this person. Even if you are not successful in obtaining a meeting, at least try to get two more contact names from this new person that you can call. Then telephone the originating contact to let him or her know how the lead worked out.

Always, always thank people for their time and efforts on your behalf, and *always* follow up how and when you indicated you would. After every meeting, send the person you met with a thank-you note. (We will examine thank-you notes later on in this chapter.) Actively keep your network going. Don't let your contacts drift. It takes perseverance, work, dedication, and lots of energy, but networking is worth it in more ways than one:

1. You may find a job.
2. You will be out and meeting new people.
3. You'll have something to look forward to and feel positive about.
4. These meetings and calls can boost your self-confidence and make you feel more positive because you are taking action. You are being proactive and in control, instead of just passively waiting for your letters to arrive or a headhunter to call you.
5. Meeting with people is good practice for actual job interviews.
6. If you are referred to someone and there is a job opening, you will have an advantage over the competition. The odds will be in your favour.
7. There may be a new and unannounced position and you can save the company the time and expense of going through the rigors of a search. There you are — the perfect candidate right in front of them!
8. You may impress your host so much that he or she will create a position for you. It does happen!
9. Networking can be fun.

Networking does work. That is how Stan T. got his job. Let's look at his story:

"I had been working at the same company for sixteen and a half years. I was hired in a junior position and worked my way up through the ranks to be one of the Vice-Presidents. The firm was a large international company, yet there was a real feeling of trust, closeness, and loyalty amongst the employees toward each other and toward the company. In fact, the company actively fostered this "family" feeling. I felt very comfortable and secure in my job. Then the company was sold. There was a great deal of fear. Warehouses were closed, staff was cut, and distribution networks were restructured. There were a lot of questions being asked and not many answers being offered. My division was told that it was safe. Nothing would change. I believed them. In a million years, I would never have thought that I would be one of the casualties.

"Then on Monday October 15, 1990, at 4:30 p.m. (seven months after the company was bought), I was called into the President's office. There was an Executive Vice-President — my boss — there as well. They closed the door, and before I even had a chance to sit down, I was told: 'We have some bad news for you. We're terminating your employment as of today. We are restructuring and you are not a part of the plan. We have a package put together for you. We suggest that you read it over, take it to a lawyer, and when you've done that, get back to us, and if everything is acceptable we'll finalize the deal. Sorry, but we have to move on.' *And that was it!* It was so cold, matter-of-fact, and fast. The whole thing took less than five minutes! I walked out with the envelope they gave me, totally stunned, and went back to my office in a daze. I sat down at my desk and picked up where I left off with my work. It took me a few minutes to realize what had happened. I called home and told my wife what happened and that I was coming home. I picked up my jacket and left.

"My wife was shocked, angry, upset, as hurt as I was and hurt for me. She was also very, very supportive. I was still in shock. I opened the envelope and we went through the severance package. I was given the equivalent of a year's salary in a lump sum. I went to my lawyer the next day with the package. He didn't specialize in this type of thing but he immediately got on the phone with someone who did, and they spoke for a while and went through everything. The advice that I got was that the package was a good one, and if I fought them it would cost me a lot of money, delay things, and there was no sense in it. I should sign the documents, take the money, and put this behind me and get on with my life. It was good advice and I took it. I then met with my accountant as to how to handle the money for tax advantages and then I met with my ex-company and finalized things. When I went back to the company to pick up my things, I found out that two other vice-presidents got the axe earlier that day. That made me feel better for a minute because I realized that I wasn't the only casualty. I also found out that many people in the office were very upset by my departure (I am happy to say!).

"My three children were ten, nine, and one-month-old respectively. We first told them that I'd be off work for a little while and explained it as holiday time. We let that go for a couple of days. I wasn't prepared and couldn't come to grips with the fact that I lost my job, and I certainly couldn't handle telling my children the truth. Then a few days later, I realized that I couldn't be dishonest with my kids. My wife and I sat down with them, and told them that because the company was sold, things were being changed and a number of people were losing their jobs and I was one of them. We told them not to panic because we still had lots of money. I was nervous about their reaction, but all they said was 'Hooray! We'll get to see you more now.' They were pleased and I felt relieved.

"Then I spent the next week or so feeling depressed and very sorry for myself. I stayed at home and mourned the loss of my job. I received many phone calls and that support helped me. There were also some people who I expected to call, who didn't. Some people just didn't know what to say and avoided calling. I tell you, you really find out who your friends are and the strength of people's characters. Time went on, and I realized that I couldn't continue to sit around feeling sorry for myself. I had a family to support and a career I wanted to get back on track. I thought about what I wanted to do. I looked at changing industries, but then I thought, 'I've been in this business so long, I'm respected,

I've done good work, and this is what I know and do best.' I loved what I did, so I decided to stay in the industry.

"I was invited to a Christmas party that one of my ex-collegues was hosting. I was still unemployed at the time. All the people from my old company would be there. I made the difficult decision to go. I wasn't going to let them think that I was down and out. I knew that it would be good for me to be there and talk to other people in the industry who may be in a position to help me. My ex-boss was really surprised to see me there, and went overboard in the being nice department. My wife couldn't stomach it. Luckily, we managed to get through the evening without her tossing her cookies! In fact, although the evening was tough, I had some valuable conversations there.

"I was not offered the services of relocation counselling, however, I was lucky in that my wife used to be in personnel and she knew the in's and out's of looking for a job. She helped me put together my résumé. (I didn't even remember the last time I had a résumé!) Because the best jobs are never advertised, I got some leads from my contacts and made some cold calls and sent out my résumé and had some interviews. I was very active and I made sure my name was out there. I spoke to many people and went after leads that I was told about or referred to, and spent a great deal of my time researching each opportunity in depth. Looking for a job was very hard work. It was difficult sometimes to keep at it; but my wife helped me by knowing when I needed a break and knowing when I needed a push.

"Then I got a phone call from someone in the United States who runs a company in my field, who wanted to open up an office in Canada. He had called around and my name kept coming up as a potential candidate to run the Canadian office. I know that if I had not relentlessly kept calling everyone I knew, my name would not have been on the top of everyone's mind and I would not have gotten this opportunity. I did thorough research into the company, the person who runs it, the company's product, their reputation, their competition, and their way of doing business. Then the President flew me down to the States and we talked. I was there for two days and met with all their key people. I came back to Toronto and two weeks later I was offered the job!

"Just over four months after 'Black Monday' I had a much better job. I am now the General Manager of the Canadian office. I run the show. I started the company from scratch. I found office space and took care of everything from paper clips to people. I am completely responsible for everything the company does in Canada. I am much happier, challenged, and fulfilled in this job. I am working for a boss who's style matches my own, and who has given me very wide parameters in which to do my job. I make more money, and I have very few frustrations, and I am enjoying myself!

"It is really tough to handle being dismissed from a position, especially if you have been at the same company for a long time. You feel that a big part of your life is missing. Losing your job is like losing a limb. It is really a part of you. But there is a much bigger world out there that you have to explore. You need to take the downside of everything that has happened to you, and turn it into an opportunity. Say, 'Okay, I'm free. I'm able now to pursue something that could be really interesting, different, and much better for me. ' Then you must do whatever it is that you have to do to get it. (Without hurting anyone of course.) You may not get it right away; you may have to cross a stepping stone to get there, but if you keep after your goals, you will eventually get what you want."

~

So, always network. Anyone that you meet anywhere can know someone (who knows someone) who can help you. Always be positive and confident in your communication. Networking will give you the opportunity to meet many interesting people and will keep you busy. It will also give you the opportunity to uncover and discover hidden job leads. There is one version of networking that is gaining in popularity due to its effectiveness. It is called the advice or information meeting.

THE ADVICE OR INFORMATION MEETING

"Many receive advice, only the wise profit from it."

—SYRUS

This is a particularly valuable tool if you are thinking about changing careers or industries, but it also works well under any job search circumstances. This is how it works:

Identify five to ten successful, accomplished business people that you respect and admire, and who could be in a position to help you. If you are entering a new industry and are unsure of who the movers and shakers are, be sure to do your homework first. Research the industry to find out who you should talk to. Then write a letter to these people asking for their advice and a brief meeting with them. *Do not send your résumé and do not ask for a job.* In fact, you don't even have to be specific about currently being unemployed. There is an example of an advice-seeking letter involving a career change and an example of a general information-gathering letter in the Appendix at the end of this chapter.

Once you've sent out the letter, follow up with a telephone call exactly when you indicated you would. (It should be approximately five to eight working days from the date of the letter.) Once you get your target on the telephone (which is no easy task), briefly re-state what you said in the letter and ask for a meeting. Tell your target that you will not ask for a job, try to sell anything, or take up more than twenty minutes of his or her time. Be politely persistent. Usually you will get a meeting.

When you get the meeting, arrive early and freshen up. Relax. Breathe deeply. Present yourself a few minutes early. Warmly greet your "advisor" by smiling, shaking his or her hand, and looking the person in the eye. Be confident and positive. Make sure to thank your advisor both before and after the meeting. When you get in the office, briefly state your experience and capsulize your career and ask what they would do if they were in your shoes. Or, if you are changing industries, ask what opportunities there are for someone with your qualifications in that field. Then *listen.*

If you are asked a question answer it briefly and succinctly. Keep track of the time. After you have been there for twenty minutes, note it and get ready to leave. You may be invited to stay longer. If so, be on your toes for signals that the meeting is over. Don't stay longer than one hour. At the end of the meeting ask if there is anyone that they could refer you to to further assist you in your research. Be sure to leave your "business card" (remember Chapter 1) with your new contact. In some cases your host may express interest in hiring you. That's great! But don't *you* be the one to ask for a job. Your credibility will be shot and you may jeopardize your chance at getting other referrals.

After your meeting send a thank-you note (typewritten) no later than the next day. Thank your host for sharing his or her time and advice with you and referring other contacts to you. Be sure to mention a few key things that were discussed during the meeting. (For example, "Thank you for the insights you shared with me on . . ." or "Thank you for your kind referral to Mr. . . .") Detail your follow-up plans for the contacts that you were given and tell them that you will keep them posted on further developments. Then, when you do follow up with the new contacts, call or write the originator and let him or her know how things went. Not only is that common courtesy, but it will ease the sponsor's mind that things went well (and that the referral did not reflect badly on him), and it shows that you are willing to go that extra mile. Also, something or someone else may have occurred to your advisor in the meantime. It also serves to keep your network active.

This information-gathering/advice-seeking technique gets results. The only potential drawback is that as this technique gains in popularity and the ranks of unemployed executives swell, there may be too many advice-seekers, seeking the time of these busy, successful executives. One president of a large company regretfully admitted that he gets so many requests for these types of meetings, that he cannot accept them anymore. So if you find this happening to you, find a way to put a variation on this theme. Differentiate yourself.

This technique will feel uncomfortable at first because you will be putting yourself in an uneasy, foreign situation where you have to push and stretch yourself. To get ahead in the job market today you've got to put yourself out and take risks. It will pay off in spades. It will lift your morale, and you will meet new and respected people, get good advice, have interview practice, and potentially get a lead to a job. Getting out and talking to key people is one of the best ways to hit a jackpot in the casino of unemployment.

"A single conversation across the table with a wise man is worth a month's study of books."
—CHINESE PROVERB

A case could be made that you should skip the advice-seeking letter and move directly to the telephone call. This can work if you are poised and self-assured. The downside is that you will be intruding on a senior person's day and your call may not be well-timed. The decision is yours. Do what feels best for you. However, getting through and making contact with your targets on the telephone is not easy. The following are some techniques to help you break through the telephone barrier.

TELEPHONE TIPS

Don't expect to reach your target on the telephone on your first try. (If you do, consider yourself lucky.) Not only are these senior executives busy and often not in the office or are in meetings, there are also gatekeepers (otherwise known as secretaries and assistants) who are paid to guard the time and privacy of their boss. You will need to have a winning attitude when you make the call. You should sound confident and self-assured. It is a good idea to fantasize about how the successful telephone conversation will go. (You may want to refer back to Chapter 3.) Do a practice run in your mind before you actually pick up the phone and make the call. Picture in your mind what you will say and how you will get through. This not only makes you feel more confident, but you can anticipate negative responses and plan how to get around them. You can pre-de-bug the call and keep yourself focused by limiting your fluster level.

When you do call your target and a screener answers, *always* be polite. Watch your tone of voice. Never sound irritated, exasperated, or condescending. (Not only in your job search, but in life, you should always speak to everyone you encounter with respect.) If the person you want to reach is in a meeting, out of the office, or otherwise unavailable, ask when a good time to call back would be. Don't leave your name or number. Instead say that you will be hard to reach and you will try back at the suggested time. Then do it. Probably again and again. Don't get discouraged. Keep trying. Form an alliance with the gatekeeper. If you get them on your side your chances of success are greater.

Some people suggest that when the screener asks what the call is regarding (which they usually will do), you should respond by saying that it is of a personal nature. That may get you through, but the danger with that tactic is that you got connected under false pretenses and that may irritate the person you are trying to see. Instead, you may want to respond by saying that you were hoping to speak to Mr. Important to gain valuable insight from his advice; or, you are a colleague of Ms. Big and you were calling to ask her opinion on a confidential matter. Another method for reaching a hard to get executive is to call either before or after normal working hours. There is the highest likelihood that they will answer their own phones before 8:30 a.m. and after 5:30 p.m. (as I am sure you remember from working overtime many times yourself).

How many times should you try to get through to your target? You must keep trying *until* you reach the person you want to speak to. Polite, positive persistence is the key to reaching your goals.

Many times you will feel like giving up. Don't. Maybe you can learn from Heather P.'s story:

"I graduated with my M.B.A. degree in 1979. My ticket to success! I was recruited by a bank and started in their executive training program. I was very dedicated to my career. I worked hard and put in long hours and worked most weekends. I had no social life — who had time?! I was rewarded by a steady stream of promotions up the corporate ladder. I gave a decade of my life to that bank, and then, one day, out of the blue, I was called into to my boss' office. He was with the Vice-President of Personnel. It was in the late afternoon. My boss said something about restructering, and then he said, 'We are going to have to let you go. I'm sorry.' I went numb. I kept hearing that sentence ringing over and over in my mind. They gave me a document and I was escorted to another office where I was greeted by an outplacement counsellor. It is all such a blur. I remember spending time with and talking to the counsellor. She took me to an early dinner and tried to make me feel better. My recollection of that day is really fuzzy. I was numb and in shock. I couldn't believe it really happened. I kept thinking it was all a bad dream and I would wake up soon. Things like this don't happen to people like me!

"Well, needless to say, it took me a while, but with the help of my outplacement counsellor I got myself prepared for the arduous process of looking for a job. Something that I never had to do before. I also did some soul-searching. I mean, I was in my mid-thirties, and I felt that I was a failure. I felt that I had nothing. No job. No relationship. I decided that I didn't want to continue my life as it had been. I needed and wanted a well-balanced life.

"The outplacement counsellor and I talked a lot about my goals, both personally and professionally. We ended up identifying some career options for me, none of which were in banking. I focused on two industries I wanted to break into. I researched those fields, found out what was happening in each field, who the influential people were, and what issues they faced. I spent a great deal of time in the library. With the help of the outplacement firm, I put together a résumé which focused on my skills and experience that could be transferable to a different environment and still be valuable.

"Then I wrote lots and lots of letters. I sent out my résumé, broadcast letters, and advice-seeking letters. I must have sent over 300 letters, gone to over thirty advice meetings, and about twenty interviews in one year. I had some days when I thought that I just couldn't go on. I remember one particular week, when I had to really push myself to go to an 'advice' meeting. I almost called to cancel it, but it had taken me over two weeks to get through to the person to set up the meeting, so I knew I had to go. I pumped myself up (I felt like a limp punching bag that all the air had leaked out of, and I was forcefully pumping the air back into it), and went to the meeting. As it turned out, the day before the meeting someone had just quit and the position I was looking for was available! The person I met with was impressed with me and then I met with the immediate boss of the position and we clicked. I got the job offer the next day!!

"I love my job, and the hours are not maniacal. I have a social life (I even date now, which makes my mother very happy), and I am a much happier, well-rounded person. It took a year of getting rejection after rejection, unreturned phone calls, and doors slammed in my face until I got my job. It was the most difficult period and the most enlightening period of my life. But in the end, having persevered, I am much better off from the experience and I have a fuller and richer life."

~

A Review — How To Find Job Leads

- Continually and diligently read the classified or career sections of your daily newspapers and job market sections of your trade and industry publications.

- Register with two or three top executive search firms that specialize in your industry.

- Send out your résumé and covering letters or broadcast letters to target companies (which you have researched), addressed to a specific senior person who can be in a position to hire you.

- Continually network, network, network.

- Utilize the advice-seeking/information-gathering networking tool.

- Look for leads in government directories.

- Read between the lines in business stories. Always be on the lookout for a potential opportunity.

- Look for recent appointments in the news. Congratulate the person who was promoted — who is taking over that position?

- Find target companies in the Yellow Pages.

- Read trade directories that disclose who's who.

Interviews

You may not have had to go through an interview since you got out of school. Now suddenly you are sitting on the other, unfamiliar side of the desk. You are in the hot seat. It can be a traumatic, terrifying experience. Or, it can be fun. The best antidote to fear is preparation. So make sure you have done your homework on each and every company that grants you an interview.

Research And Preparation For The Interview

"Chance favours the prepared mind."

—LOUIS PASTEUR

When you get an interview, the first thing you should do is research the company as thoroughly as you can. (I am assuming here that you have already done your basic preliminary industry and company research and you are familiar with their issues, trends, problems, and opportunities. If not, refer back to the previous section — and shame on you!)

Now you need to find out as much as you can about the company. Try to get your hands on any literature that the company puts out (brochures, annual reports, weekly newsletters) and call anyone you know who might have information about the company (suppliers, clients, former or current employees). Look at their advertising. What is their message? Try to find out the personality, philosophy, general direction, financial situation, stability, growth potential, dress code, strengths, weaknesses, size, products, services, competition, key executives, plant locations, track record, ownership, reputation, and anything else you can about the company. Also try to find out as much as you can about the person who will be interviewing you. Has he made any speeches lately? On what? Have the media interviewed her lately? What are her views? What are his hot buttons?

Now you are an informed, knowledgeable candidate. One who will stand out because you can speak their language and understand and address their needs and concerns. You are able to set yourself up to solve their problems. Your preparation will give you knowledge and your knowledge will give you confidence. Don't expect to pass the test if you haven't done your homework!

As additional preparation for your interview, fantasize how the perfect interview will go in your mind. Imagine the interviewer being friendly. You hit it off immediately. You play their questions and your self-assured answers over and over in your mind. You anticipate and are ready for even the most difficult questions. You picture the interview ending successfully. You walk out smiling and feeling great.

Aside from mental practice, it is also a good idea to actively practise your interview skills. Get a tape recorder and record your answers and see how you sound. Ask a good friend or your spouse to do a mock interview with you and tape it. An audio tape will do; but if you can use video tape that is even better, because not only will you be able to hear how you sound, but you will be able to see how you come across. Remember how important your body language and tonality is in communicating? If not refer back to Chapter 3.

Here is an audio check list:

- Does your voice sound confident, self-assured, and positive, or do you sound depressed, negative, or condescending?

- Do you hmm and uhh too much?

- Are you using proper voice inflection? For example, if you are asking a question your voice will go up at the end of a sentence. If you are making a statement or responding to a question, your voice should not have that same inflection. That makes you seem unsure of yourself.

- Are you talking too softly or too loudly?

- Did you swear by mistake and not realize it until you heard the tape played back? If so, watch out. An interview is not the place to display colourful language. Not even to make a point.

- Do you tend to cut the "interviewer" off? Let the other person finish their sentences and their train of thought.

- Did you really listen to the question? Was your answer direct, relevant, and to the point?

Here is a video check list:

- Watch your posture. Are you standing and sitting straight with your shoulders back? Do you look stiff or at ease?

- Are you leaning slightly in, as opposed to sitting far back in your chair?

- Do you have any nervous ticks, are you fidgeting, or do you use big exaggerated gestures when speaking?

- Are you smiling most of the time? (Don't plaster a fake smile on your face, but do try to smile as much as you can.)

- Are you maintaining good eye contact? (Don't go overboard and stare down your interviewer.)

- Are your arms crossed tightly around your chest (in a defensive posture) or are they relaxed on your lap?

- Do you come across as friendly, professional, confident and enthusiastic?

Remember, practice makes perfect!

Dress For Success

Your image and how you come across is greatly affected by your appearance. You must make sure that you groom and dress yourself appropriately for the industry, corporate culture, and the job itself. If, for example, you are in a creative industry, you will have more leeway and flexibility in your attire. However, here are some standard helpful hints in projecting the proper, professional image:

- Don't eat a Caesar salad or anything very garlicy the night before or the day of your interview. It will be evident in your breath and it will come out in your pores the next day.

- Shower before your interview if you can. You will feel fresh and it will guard against body odour.

- Make sure your breath is fresh, your teeth are clean (no poppy seeds stuck there from your morning bagel), nails are well manicured (ladies — no chipped or flashy-coloured polish; men — no rough hangnails and be sure to have clean fingernails), and your hair is freshly washed and neat.

- Never wear boots in an interview. Bring a pair of good shoes and change into them in the reception area. Also, make sure that your shoes are polished and clean. (Black or navy coloured shoes are best. Men — no loafers; and ladies — low heels and closed toe and heel.)

- Go easy (if at all) on perfume, cologne, and after shave.

- Always wear a comfortable, good quality "power" suit. It should preferably be navy blue or grey and worn with a light- coloured shirt.

- Men — your socks should match your shoes, pants or tie.

- Women — your pantyhose should match your skirt.
  - do not wear patterned hose.
  - bring an extra pair of hose in case you get a run.
  - do not wear pants.
  - do not wear clunky jewelry.
  - no heavy or overdone make-up.

The nineties is a decade of polish. Your image and your appearance will determine to a large extent, how you are perceived and will have a great impact on the first impression you make. The importance of first impressions cannot be underestimated. Give yourself every advantage you can. Dress for success and you will feel successful.

Final Preparation

"Luck is what happens when preparation meets opportunity."

—Elmer Letterman

Before you go for your interview, try to relax. Do some relaxation exercises before you leave home. Do some deep breathing. Then give yourself plenty of time to get to your destination in case you run into a traffic jam, a closed road, or you discover that your directions are wrong. On your way to the interview, listen to your favourite radio station (but avoid the news) or one of your favorite tapes. You may also want to listen to a motivational cassette or the tape you made with your positive affirmations on it. Or you may want to be quiet and run over the interview one final time in your mind. Make the ride there as enjoyable and stress-free as possible. Then, when you arrive you will feel at your best.

If you've given yourself extra time at the outset and haven't gotten lost or hit a traffic snarl, you will arrive early. Find a washroom and freshen up. Do some deep breathing, smile and then approximately five minutes before the appointed time, present yourself to the receptionist. Always be polite and friendly to the receptionist. Not only is that good manners and proper behaviour, but also, sometimes receptionists are asked for their opinion of you, or the receptionist may be on break and the person there is really the boss' secretary (who you want on your side). If it is winter, leave your coat and boots at the reception area and change into your shoes. You are now ready for that moment of truth. Oh yes, and one more thing:

Expect the unexpected!

The Interview

Greet your interviewer warmly. Shake hands firmly, look them in the eye and smile. Comment on something (the weather, the office, something unique you noticed) to break the ice and set a pleasant tone. The interviewer will generally point out where you should sit. Sit up straight — don't slouch — and *you're ready.*

You are going to be judged on how you present yourself in addition to what you say. You are a total package consisting of:

- your appearance: suit, shoes, and other attire
  hair, nails, and jewelry
  your overall physical look

- personal hygiene: fresh breath
  clean teeth
  washed hair
  body odour (that is, lack of body odour!)

- your attitude: positive
  enthusiastic
  energetic
  confident and self-assured
  business-like and professional
  style

- your presentation: well-spoken
  personable/friendly
  what you say and how you say it
  body language/physiology
  voice patterns
  communication ability

First impressions are critical. The interviewer will have formulated an impression of you in the first five minutes of meeting you. (Some people say an impression is formed within the first seven seconds!) If it is a positive impression, you will have the advantage of being under the halo effect for the rest of the interview. If, on the other hand, it is a negative impression, the interview may be more of a struggle as you must work hard to negate that first impression.

Interview Procedures

There are two agendas at play in an interview situation.

1. The employer wants to know about you. Who you are, what you have to offer, what motivates you, can you do the job, will you fit in, can you grow within the organization?

2. You want to know about the job. Is it a match with your values, beliefs, skills, interests, and goals? What are the people you would work with like? What is expected of you? Is there opportunity for growth?

Remember, it is a two-way communication process. (It may be less intimidating if you think of the interview as a business meeting.) Some interviews are more structured than others. Some may have a definite agenda and others may flow more loosely and freely. Some interviews may take place over coffee or lunch, and others happen in an office environment. Some interviewers will be more skilled at interviewing than others. Basically, it is hard to predict how your interview will go. However, there are some general do's and don'ts to follow for a successful interview.

Do:

- Try to establish rapport with the interviewer by matching and mirroring their body language, vocal pace, and tone.

- Look for areas of commonality. (You may want to refer back to Chapter 3 to refresh yourself on these rapport-building tips.)

- Make sure you really, actively *listen* to what is being said and asked, and then respond directly, clearly, briefly, and positively.

- Always try to relate your statements and answers back to the needs of the job at hand.

- If you are unsure of a question, ask for clarification. Don't guess.

- Discuss your skills in terms of accomplishments and successes. Tell mini-stories that highlight the results you've achieved, and relate that back to the job requirements.
- Maintain good eye contact (but don't stare).
- Maintain good posture.
- Be friendly, yet professional. Smile when it is appropriate.
- Speak clearly and articulately in a positive, confident manner. (If you don't feel confident, act as if you do.)
- Ask questions that are relevant and showcase your knowledge about the industry and the company.
- At the end of the interview, re-state your interest in the position, ask what the next steps are, and thank the interviewer for their time.

Do Not:

- address the interviewer by first name, unless you are specifically invited to do so.
- argue with your interviewer — under any circumstances.
- be arrogant or condescending in your manner or your tone.
- fidget or engage in nervous or large gestures.
- avert your eyes.
- slouch.
- mumble.
- evade the issue of age. If asked about your age, and you are concerned that you may be too old, turn a negative into a positive by capitalizing on the benefits of age. (For example, you are experienced, stable, settled, and reliable.)
- be apologetic for any of your shortcomings.
- ask irrelevant questions just for the sake of asking a question.

- Never ever criticize any former employers, co-workers, or subordinates.
- *Never* lie about your credentials.

Tips For Lunch Interviews

- If you are not directed otherwise, let your host lead the way to the table.
- Order something that is easy to eat. (Avoid spaghetti, spinach, french onion soup etc.)
- Decide quickly on your order and don't change your mind.
- Don't smoke even if your host does.
- Don't order any alcohol even if your host does. That includes wine and beer.
- Eat quickly and be ready to talk. Don't talk with your mouth full.
- Brush up on your table manners and use them.

Your goal for any interview is to get the job offer (or to at least stay in the game and be invited back for the next round). Always keep sight of your objective. It will help you to stay on track. The interview procedure usually entails an initial screening interview and then a process of interviews until a hiring decision is made. Sometimes a hiring decision is made on the second interview; whereas, other times you may have to go through numerous interviews. Basically a hiring crew will try to assess your:

experience	motivations	initiative
skills	technical abilities	leadership
fit with organization	intelligence	flexibility
ability to do the job	style	creativity
communication skills	energy	interpersonal skills
ability to learn	confidence	growth potential
self-knowledge	personality	conflict resolution
training	values	responsibility

In order to fulfill their agenda, the interviewers will ask you a number of questions. Although each interviewer is different and it is impossible to predict exactly what will take place, or what will be asked, there are certain types of questions that you can expect.

1. There are direct closed-ended questions that require a brief, concise, to-the-point answer.

2. There are open-ended questions that give you leeway in answering. Make sure to structure your answer in an organized way in relation to filling the needs of the job at hand. Discuss your achievements and how they relate to the job. Include the results and benefits of your successes.

3. There are also probing questions which may be uncomfortable and difficult to answer. If you can anticipate these questions in advance and prepare for them, you reduce your chances of being caught off guard.

To get you thinking about and anticipating how the interview might go, here is a list of some commonly asked questions (some have some suggestions on how you may want to respond; others leave it up to you).

COMMONLY ASKED INTERVIEW QUESTIONS

1. What are your strengths and weaknesses?
   Discuss three or four of your strengths (and you are familiar with them now because you have completed Chapter 4, right?), as they relate to the job, and give concrete eamples of when you demonstrated those strengths to achieve something.

2. What do you know about our company?
   Here is an opportunity to showcase what you have learned. Be careful not to come across as a know-it-all, but do sound informed, knowledgeable, and intelligent. This is where the hours of research pay off!

3. What salary are you looking for?
   Be careful here. Try to throw the ball back in their court. If that doesn't work, and they persist, you may

want to mention a salary range, or use your last salary as a benchmark. If you are negotiable on salary for the right opportunity, be sure to mention that.

4. Tell me about yourself.
   Briefly outline your background, education, career history, and discuss your achievements and successes and relate them to the job. (It is not advisable to tell the interviewer the unedited story of your life!)

5. Why did you leave your last job?
   This can be a touchy question. If your previous employer went bankrupt, or if you were squeezed out due to a downsizing or restructuring of the company, although it might be difficult to talk about it, your answer can be straightforward and the reason for leaving is understandable (especially in a tough economic climate). If, however, there was a personality conflict involved, or you still harbour some resentment and bitterness toward your ex-employer — leave that at home! No matter what, do not talk negatively about your former company, boss, or colleagues. Not even if the interviewer seems sympathetic to you. Hopefully you got your exit story straight with your ex-employer, so stick to that. Practise your own answer to that question out loud, so that you can feel more comfortable with saying it.

6. What were some of the problems you faced in your career and how did you handle them?
   This is the time to highlight your problem-solving, interpersonal, and communication skills. Also try to show creativity and ingenuity in problem-solving. Give concrete examples.

7. Why do you want to join this company? Why do you want this job?

Showtime! This a great arena in which to display
your knowledge. Again, the research pays off.

8. Why do you want to make this career change?
You should definitely be clear on this in your
own mind. Don't ramble. Answer as succinctly
as possible.

9. What do you look for in an employer? A job?
Again, your research (both on yourself — wants and
needs; and on the company) is worth it.

10. What have you done that you are most proud of in
your career and in your personal life?
This is a great opportunity to showcase your talents,
but be sure to relate your answer to the job you are
interviewing for.

11. What would your ideal job be?
You already identified this in Chapter 4; however,
temper your answer to be consistent with the job
at hand.

12. Why have you had so many jobs?
If you have jumped around a lot be prepared for
this one.

13. What would you do if . . . ?
For these type of hypothetical questions show your
thinking process to problem-solving. You may not
have the "right" answer but if your thought process
is sound you are safe.

14. Why should we hire you?
Sales pitch time.

15. What are you motivated by?

16. What do you look for in the people you hire?

17. What do you do in your leisure time?

18. If we called your former boss/peers/subordinates
what would they say about you?

19. What other jobs are you considering?

20. If you were starting all over again, what job career would you pick?
21. Where do you want to be in five years?
22. What kind of decisions are the hardest/easiest for you to make?
23. Describe your management style.
24. What style do you prefer in a boss?
25. Are you available to travel or relocate?
26. What would your spouse or best friend say about you? Would you agree or disagree?
27. Have you ever thought about going into business for yourself? (More about this in the next section.)

The other agenda of an interview situation is yours. You need to ask questions to find out more about the job and what would be expected of you, and you also will want to ask questions to demonstrate your knowledge (gained from all your research). Make sure that your questions are well thought out and relevant. That is not to say that you have to pre-plan all of your questions in advance, but when you are asking a spontaneous question think about it before you ask it. Asking a frivolous or silly question can hurt you more than not asking any questions at all. Of course the questions you ask should be your own and geared specifically to each opportunity. Focus in on a hot issue, concern, or trend that is facing the industry or company and ask about how that is affecting how they do business. Be sure to show interest and enthusiasm. Save questions on salary, vacation, benefits, and stock options until you have a firm job offer.

Wind Down

After the interview, review what happened. Assess how you did. Was there anything that went particularly well? Was there anything that you should make sure you don't do again? What can you improve on for next time? Even a bad interview can be a positive experience if you can learn from it. Practice makes perfect. Keep practicing your interviewing skills both in your mind and with a good friend or your spouse. Go to as many interviews as possible. Even go to job interviews that you are not really interested in. It will be good practice and, who knows, you may change your mind or at least get another lead!

Follow Up

After the interview, you should write a brief, typewritten thank-you letter to the person or people who interviewed you. The letter should be sent out by the next day. The thank-you letter should be personalized — addressed specifically to the person who interviewed you — and should comment on an issue or topic of conversation that came up during the interview. Take this opportunity to again stress your suitability for the job by highlighting what you think are your key skills and abilities as they relate to and meet the needs of the job. Add any details that you feel are relevant that you may have forgotten to mention during the interview. Refer to the next steps that were agreed to during the interview and thank the interviewer for their time and re-state your interest in the position. Don't forget to date and sign the letter.

Then you have to wait. The waiting is difficult. Try to keep busy and occupy your mind with other things (such as your next letter, meeting, interview), so you don't fixate on the wait. If you haven't heard from the company by a week past the set follow-up date, call the interviewer and politely ask about the status of the situation. Try not to get too excited about any particular job possibility, because if you don't get the job your disappointment will be overwhelming, and it will be hard to get back on the job search track.

Even if a job offer seems imminent, never stop your job search, until you have a *firm* offer. Don't let other possibilities pass you by while you wait for that almost certain job that in the last minute falls through. Keep as many irons red-hot in the fire as you can. It is unrealistic to expect that you will get every job that you interview for, so prepare for and expect some rejection.

Most of the time if you get passed over for a job it was for the best. Perhaps another candidate was more qualified than you, or maybe there just was not a good match between you and the company or the job. Don't take it as a personal rejection. If you don't get a job that you really wanted, and that you felt was a good fit with you, call up the interviewer and politely ask why you did not get the position. If you explain that you are asking for your own education and development, most people will be honest with you. Then take that feedback and learn from it.

References

You will need to identify three or four people who have worked with you in the past (preferably former employers), who will speak highly of your skills, abilities, and personality, and give you a good recommendation. Be sure to call each person that you select as a reference and ask them if they would mind being listed as a reference for you and would they honestly give you a good testimonial. Once you have your list of references, on a separate sheet of the same paper stock as you are using for your letters, type out your reference list. This catalog of references should include the person's name, company, title, and work phone number.

It is a good idea to send each reference a copy of your résumé to serve as a refresher in terms of your experience and your strengths and accomplishments. After you have been asked for your references by an interested company, call each reference and let them know that Mr. X from ABC company will be calling for a reference on you for _____ job. Then tell each reference about the company, the job, your opinion about both, and what you think the interviewer will be looking for. Then ask your references to call you if they are contacted by the potential employer. Don't forget to thank them.

If you happen to go through a long stretch without getting to the point of being asked for your references, keep in touch with your references anyway. Call them to advise them of the status of your job search. Maybe they have thought of a new lead? Keep in touch with these people. After you do get a job, make sure that you write a thank-you letter to each reference and inform them about your new job.

Evaluating the Job Offer

Well, you did it!!! You got the job offer!! Good for you! Don't get so excited that you can't think clearly. Make sure that you carefully evaluate the job and the offer. Sometimes you may get a job offer that is not exactly what you wanted, but you've been out of work for awhile and this is the only offer that you have received. It is not always easy to decide whether or not you should accept the job. Evaluate the job offer against what you want. Refer back to the job criteria you established in Chapter 4.

- Is the salary close to what you want or feel you are worth?
- What are the working conditions?
- What is the corporate culture like?
- Will you fit in?

Don't accept just any job or the first job that comes along without giving it considerable consideration, because if the job does not meet your needs, and is wrong for you, you will be miserable, unmotivated, and you ultimately won't last long. That means you may have to face a job search all over again. Here are some *wrong* reasons for accepting a job offer:

- pressure (financial, emotional, family).
- pride.

- impatience with the job search.
- panic that you won't get another offer.
- "It's a job and at least it's work" attitude.

Take all these factors into consideration and then make your decision. Make sure it is a rational, calm, objective judgement. If you have to take a job due to financial reasons, then you must. Only you (and your family) know your priorities, your resources, and your limits. Discuss the offer with your family or closest friend. Talk it over with someone who knows you well. Get their opinion. Then make the decision that is best for you.

If you do decide to accept the job offer, don't be afraid to negotiate. For example if the salary offered is lower than you'd like, you may be able to bargain for non-cash compensation (stock options, bonus plan, etc.). The key is to be flexible, know the outcome you want, and look for ways to get what you want while keeping the other party happy as well. (More will be said about negotiating skills in Chapter 6.)

Tie It Up

When your job search is over (thank heaven!), and you have accepted your new position, call or write all the people who were helpful to you in your search. Call those that you know best and write to the others. Thank them for their help and inform them of your new position. Fight the inclination to destroy all of the evidence of your job search. Don't throw away or burn any of your job search records. You should have a great deal of information compiled that took a lot of work and sweat. File it away. Keep in touch with and cultivate the contacts you had and established during your search. Then, if the unthinkable ever (heaven forbid!) happens again, you will be well prepared.

Doing It Your Way — Starting Your Own Business

"Small opportunities are often the beginning of great enterprises. "

— DEMOSTHENES

Have you ever thought about starting your own business? This is an option that you may want to seriously consider. You may want to go into business for yourself because:

- You'd never have to worry about being fired or laid off again.
- You would be your own boss.
- You would have independence and flexibility.
- You would call the shots.
- You'd be the master of your own destiny.
- No more being humble and kowtowing to the powers that be.
- You would have an unlimited earning potential — *you could get rich!!!*

You may be fed up with your job search. You may not have been able to find a job. You may have a great idea for a new product or service that you've always had to keep on the back burner due to your other (more pressing) priorities. You may have always dreamed about having your own business. You may be tired of working hard for someone else's financial benefit.

These are all powerful motivating and justifiable reasons for deciding to go into business for yourself. However, before you dive head-first into the alluring ocean of entrepreneurship, stop and check the water. Look out for the dangers of unknown territory. There are risks and pitfalls to be aware of when you are considering starting your own business. There will be no more security and predictability of pay cheques, no supplied administrative support, office facilities and equipment, and no health plan benefits. Also keep in mind that more new businesses fail than succeed, and it takes *long* hours, *hard* work, and a great deal of *dedication* to make a new business flourish.

"Genius is one percent inspiration and ninety-nine percent perspiration."
— Thomas Edison

Not everyone is cut out to be an entrepreneur. You've got to examine yourself closely.

- Are you a risk-taker?
- Do you have an abundance of energy?
- Are you a good decision-maker?
- Are you a self-starter and self-motivated?
- Are you flexible, adaptable, creative, enterprising, innovative and resourceful?
- Are you disciplined and responsible?
- Do you have a lot of confidence and enthusiasm?
- Are you never satisfied with the status quo?
- Are you very persistent, and do you persevere against all odds?
- Do you have an idea, product, or service that is marketable?
- A key consideration is, do you have enough money? (Your severance settlement may suit that purpose very nicely.)

Make sure that you have enough capital to finance your business start-up and operation costs and personal expenses for a year without counting on any income. You must therefore know the cost of setting up and running your business and determine the capital needed *before* you begin. You must do a cash flow analysis. Look at what your initial costs will be, your daily operating costs, your fixed and variable costs, and your estimated revenue. It is imperative that you do proper financial planning before you jump into a new venture. Some sources of funding are:

- your severance.
- your savings.
- loans from family or friends (be careful here!).
- investors/venture capitalists.
- banks.
- government loans and grants (federal and provincial) and the Federal Business Development Bank.
- lines of credit from suppliers.

There are three ways to own your business:

1. **START FROM SCRATCH.** This is the classic entrepreneurial situation. The potential risks and rewards are highest, and there is the most amount of personal freedom in determining what the business will be and where it will go. You will need to create a company name, identification, image, and logo. You will need to have a viable, marketable idea, product, or service. (If you have a hobby, interest or passion about something and can turn that into your business venture, all the better.) You should test the feasibility and need for your business. Identify a target market. Research the competition. Know what you are getting into. The more you know, the better off you are. You should have the entrepreneurial personality traits that were outlined above for a better chance of success.

   "Do not follow where the path may lead. Go instead where there is no path and leave a trail."
   —ANONYMOUS

2. **BUY A COMPANY.** There two ways to do this:

   a) *An Asset Purchase*: entails buying the assets of a company and the company name, free and clear of any liens on the business.

   b) *A Share Purchase*: entails taking over the business exactly as it is, which means you assume the liabilities too.

Be sure to do *thorough* research before you commit to a company purchase of any kind! Make sure that you have a clear understanding of why the company is for sale, what the business is really worth, and what you will do with it to make it a success. Is there growth potential? Look at current and recent financial statements, and client/customer and supplier lists. There is less risk involved going this route, as relationships are already established with suppliers, bankers, and customers.

3. If you want to run your own business, but are averse to risk-taking, and are not comfortable with hazarding into the unknown, and do not have a stellar idea, then **FRANCHISING** may be ideal for you. You get the freedom of being self-employed *and* the security of working for an established company. You have support and training, and the risk of failure is minimized. (But remember, you must do your research, and even then, there are no guarantees.) If you are a typical entrepreneur, franchising may not be for you, because you must agree to fit into an established system, accept rules and regulations, and be a team player. However, the franchising option would be a perfect fit for a manager-type personality. Buying a franchise means buying into an established way of operating a business. You buy the whole package. No innovators need apply. You must adhere to the franchisor's formula for success. Again, be sure to do your research before you invest in anything. *Caveat emptor* — Let the buyer beware!

Whether you are starting a new business from scratch, buying a company, or purchasing a franchise, it is imperative that you see a lawyer and an accountant before making any final decisions. It will be money well spent to purchase expertise that could prevent you from making very costly mistakes.

Solo Or Duet

There is also the question of whether you want to be a sole proprietor, or have one or more partners. When you fly solo, you will make all the decisions yourself, answer to no one (well, maybe your banker), and gain all the profits or suffer all the losses. If you decide to take a partner, you must have a partnership agreement drawn up. (A lawyer will do this for you.) You will then become responsible for your partner's actions. This is a very important point. You could be sued due to what your partner does, so pick your partner(s) carefully. With a partner, you will have someone to bounce ideas off, share the work load with, and share the losses with. You must also share the profits, and discuss decisions and directions for the business (and work out conflicting ideas), with your partner. You should strike up a partnership with someone who has what you lack. For example, you may have the idea; your partner may have the money; or you may have one set of skills, and your partner should have a complementary, not similar, set of skills.

> *"When two men in a business always agree, one of them is unnecessary."*
>
> —UNKNOWN

The Business Plan

Once you have decided what you want to do, you will need to put together a *business plan*.

Your business plan is a document that outlines:

- what your business is/your idea, product, or service.
- the goals and objectives for the business (including a time frame).
- an analysis of the market including the competition.
- the sources and uses of funds.
- financial analysis — budget, cash flow projection, break-even analysis.

- the marketing strategy — needs, target market, promotion, distribution, etc.
- production plans if applicable.
- organization of the company.
- your background.

If you are using your business plan to secure a loan, make sure you also include any collateral you may have and how and when you would re-pay the loan. (By the way, it is a good idea to try to establish an alliance with your banker. A good relationship with the one who has the access to funds can be of immeasurable help to you.)

Going into business for yourself always involves some risk. However, if you plan carefully, test your ideas, do extensive and thorough research, and use the expertise of professionals, you will increase your chances of success. Running your own business is not for everyone. It will involve hard work, dedication, and a strong belief and conviction in what you are doing. It will also take up a great deal of your time. It will not be a nine-to-five situation. Make sure you discuss your intentions with your family, as it will surely have an impact upon them as well. But having your own business can also be very exciting, satisfying, fulfilling, and rewarding!

There are numerous books available on all aspects of starting and running your own business. Make sure that you know what is involved before you begin, and get help and guidance as you go along. Be sure to check into government assistance and information programs. (For instance, in Ontario, you can get a great deal of useful information by dialing, 1-800-567-2345 to reach the Small Business Start-Up Hotline.)

> *"Progress always involves risk; you can't steal second base and keep your foot on first."*
> —Frederick Wilcox

A Case In Point

Let's look at how being fired led David P. to start his own business and see the success that he enjoyed from that decision:

"I worked in radio for about ten years at the top radio station in a major market. Over the years I was a producer, music director, and on the air. I loved the radio business. Even at college, I worked at the college radio station. When I graduated, I got the job at the station by hanging around and being there to do any little job, and self-educating myself through absorption. I got offered a part-time job at first and then I turned that into a full-time job. I loved my job! In fact, some years I worked 365 days solid without any break — and enjoyed it! Radio was my life. I couldn't imagine ever doing anything else. I became the golden-haired boy and I was marked for big things.

"Then there were a number of palace coups at the station. A number of people that I felt great affection for and were mentors to me either got fired, or were significantly and abrasively demoted. I didn't like that and I let my feelings be known. Therefore, I quickly lost my golden-haired status and I became one of the enemy. Then it was me who got the bad treatment.

"I started to see the writing on the wall, so I began to do some freelance work producing sound tracks for audio-visual programs for a graphics company. (I got the job because one of the sales people at that company worked part-time at the radio station.) Through that job I did more and more freelance work, as the relations between myself and the program director got worse and worse. (He was someone that I used to be very close with.) When my contract came up for renewal I got a registered letter (which I have framed hanging on my wall to this day), basically saying that my contract would not be renewed due to a reorganization at the station. I never set foot in the station again. I mailed them my keys and I asked them to send me my personal things.

"I expected that to happen, so it didn't come as a complete shock; but there is always some heart thumping when you actually read the words. It is so real and final. I realized that it was time to assess my options. Radio had lost its appeal for me, so I thought about changing careers. I decided to focus on the freelance work I was doing, and turn that into my full-time job. In other words, I decided to go into business for myself. I had never been much of a saver, so when I got chopped I had the next month's rent and that was all. I had to hustle! I went out on the road in my sincere blue suit and using my contacts I sold my services. I sold anything in the communications and advertising field that I could think of. I was very aggressive in going after business. I got offered a few jobs with companies that I did jobs for, and I got a job offer from another radio station, but I decided to be my own boss and declined all offers and incorporated my own company.

"I lived as cheaply as I could (putting off exotic vacations and luxuries), and I worked out of the extra bedroom in my apartment. I decided to specialize in the field of corporate communications. Over the next fifteen years I took on different partners (each partner gave the business a different perspective and a fresh feel), got office space, worked very hard and watched the business grow and grow. I now run a twenty million dollar a year business, which incorporates five companies each specializing in one segment of the corporate communication business. It is the largest company in this field in Canada. I absolutely love what I do. It offers me incredible diversity, and allows for the expression of my creativity.

"Being fired started me out along my path to success. If that didn't happen, inertia would have kept me in radio and I would not have been as fulfilled as I am now. I am in control of my own destiny and I am involved in leading edge things and I am very passionate about my life. One of the keys to my success is that I never lost sight of what it was I did in my previous job that could be applicable in my next job. I never dismissed, erased, or devalued all that I learned and gained from my previous job just because I was angry that I was fired. I realized that it was valuable experience that could be applicable to my next opportunity. I always looked for new ways to use my knowledge and experiences. I recognized what I *really* did, I was not blinded or limited by what my job title said that I did."

~

Good luck and don't forget . . . look before you leap!!

Consulting And Contract Work

Another option is to do contract or consulting work to bridge the gap between your old job and your next move. There are many advantages to contract and consulting work:

- it will pay the bills.
- you will have the inside track on jobs that come available in the companies you work for, and you will also know what working in that company is like.
- you will develop many new contacts, skills, and experiences.
- you will have flexibility.
- you will be working and contributing and therefore your self-esteem and self-confidence will get a boost.
- some companies may be willing to offer you a contract or consulting job, but are not ready to commit to a full-time position.

However, the downside is that consulting and contract work involves living project to project. You may never be sure just what your income or jobs will be a year in advance (or sometimes a month in advance). Nor does this type of employment offer benefits and sick days, but it is an alternative. You may decide to do consulting or contract work while still looking for a full-time position to help cover expenses. Or you may decide to choose this as your permanent mode of employment. Whatever the case may be, make sure you know what you have to offer. Research the competition to see what they charge. Can you offer something unique?! Are you meaner or leaner?

Know your options, go after what you want, keep at it!

"The people who get on in this world are the people who get up and look for the circumstances they want, and, if they can't find them, make them."

—George Bernard Shaw

Appendix

Action Words

accelerated	controlled	formulated
accomplished	converted	founded
acquired	co-ordinated	generated
achieved	created	governed
administered	decreased	guided
advised	defined	handled
analyzed	delivered	headed
applied	demonstrated	helped
approved	designed	hired
assembled	determined	identified
assessed	developed	illustrated
assumed	devised	implemented
attained	diagnosed	improved
audited	directed	improvised
broadened	discovered	inaugurated
budgeted	displayed	increased
built	distributed	initiated
calculated	drafted	inspected
chaired	doubled	installed
capitalized	earned	instituted
charted	edited	instructed
clarified	elected	insured
coached	eliminated	interacted
collaborated	encouraged	interfaced
completed	enhanced	interpreted
composed	established	intensified
computed	estimated	introduced
conceived	exceeded	invented
conducted	expanded	investigated
conserved	expedited	launched
consolidated	evaluated	lectured
constructed	facilitated	led
contracted	focused	lessened
contributed	forecast	located

maintained	purchased	streamlined
managed	realized	strengthened
measured	recognized	stressed
maneuvered	recommended	stretched
maximized	recorded	structured
mediated	recovered	succeeded
merged	recruited	summarized
minimized	redesigned	superseded
moderated	reduced	supervised
monitored	regulated	supplied
motivated	reorganized	supported
negotiated	repaired	surpassed
obtained	represented	systematized
observed	researched	targeted
opened	reshaped	taught
operated	restored	terminated
optimized	restructured	tested
organized	retrieved	timed
originated	revamped	traced
outlined	reviewed	tracked
oversaw	revised	traded
performed	revitalized	trained
persuaded	saved	transferred
pinpointed	scheduled	transformed
planned	selected	translated
prepared	served	trimmed
prescribed	serviced	tripled
presented	set up	turned around
preserved	simplified	unified
prevented	slashed	united
prioritized	sold	unraveled
processed	solved	updated
produced	sorted	used
programmed	sparked	utilized
promoted	spearheaded	vacated
propelled	spurred	verified
proposed	staffed	won
proved	stabilized	worked
provided	started	wrote

Chronological Résumé

John Doe

ADDRESS:

PHONE:

1000 Street Crescent
Cityville, Provinceland
Q8L 3W7
(222) 555-7777 (Residence)

EDUCATION:

HARD UNIVERSITY
Graduated: 1975
Degree: M.B.A.

FUN UNIVERSITY
Graduated: 1973
Degree: B.A.
            Psychology

EMPLOYMENT HISTORY:

September 1986 – August 1991

ABC COMPANY
Director of Marketing

RESPONSIBILITIES/ACCOMPLISHMENTS:

- had total and direct responsibility for planning, developing, implementing and administering all marketing activities.
- managed an annual budget of twenty million dollars, and directed and trained a staff of five managers.
- investigated the export potential of AAA products into foreign markets, resulting in a comprehensive marketing plan for penetration of the U.S.A. market and England.
- directed the development, introduction, and implementation of a range of successful product re-launches, line extensions, product improvements, and consumer promotions.
- successfully launched a new product into the marketplace:
  — overachieved volume objective (25% over plan)
  — excelled over planned payback expectation (eight months versus one year for full return on investment).
- initiated and implemented a private label program.
- developed and managed a public relations campaign due to the closure of a main manufacturing plant.
- initiated cost improvement programmes for two products resulting in net savings of over $200m.
- reported to the President.

April 1981 – September 1986   XYZ FIRM INC.
                                     Marketing Manager

RESPONSIBILITIES/ACCOMPLISHMENTS:

- developed, communicated and executed the company's annual strategic marketing plans.
- created and implemented a national promotion program that exceeded planned objectives in coupon redemption, volume generation and market share.
- designed multi-brand promotions, prepacks, and merchandising aids for use at store level.
- developed and executed presentations for the national sales force.
- identified a need for, and developed trial-sized packages, and initiated gift-with-purchase program, and direct mail campaign.
- managed the reformulation of product X and the redesign of its packaging and spearheaded the advertising campaign to announce these changes.
- managed a staff of three.
- repositioned and relaunched XXX into national distribution resulting in a first year return on investment over plan by 15%.

June 1975 – April 1981   QRS LIMITED
                                     Brand Manager
                                     (1977 –1981)

                                     Brand Assistant
                                     (1975 –1977)

RESPONSIBILITIES/ACCOMPLISHMENTS:

- co-ordinated all day-to-day marketing activities.
- responsible for the development and training of a brand assistant.
- analyzed market trends and proposed recommendations that were accepted by management and beneficial to the HHH product category.
- initiated changes to media plan and creative strategy which increased tested awareness.
- prepared and presented comprehensive business reviews and brand plans.

HOBBIES AND INTERESTS: Travel, Tennis, Golf, Mountain Climbing, Playing Saxophone, Skiing, Stamp Collecting

FLUENT IN: English, French and Spanish

REFERENCES AVAILABLE UPON REQUEST

Functional Résumé

Mary Smith
222 Drive Road South
Bigcity, Province
Z7M 9L6
(111) 444-1234

*A SKILLED MANAGER WITH OVER 15 YEARS OF ADMINISTRATIVE
EXPERIENCE IN LARGE MULTINATIONAL COMPANIES WITH SPECIAL
STRENGTHS IN THE COMPUTER AREA.*

SKILLS
Management/
Administration

Finance

ACCOMPLISHMENTS
- Managed departments of 5–20 people.
- Won the Manager of the Year Award 5 years in a row.
- Motivated and led a special development team to successfully launch a new management system, which led to increased employee satisfaction and efficiency.
- Negotiated the lease for a new office site.
- Organized company-wide conferences and conventions that were well received.

- Responsible for preparation and management of operating and capital budgets up to $25 million.
- Analyzed financial reports and identified a cost-cutting measure that when implemented saved the company $200,000 per year.
- Designed a computerized financial reporting system which increased company efficiency.

Marketing	• Initiated media contact to launch a new product, which generated a great amount of positive publicity and resulted in initial sales of 20% over plan. • Hosted a sales meeting and acted as spokesperson to announce the company's plans for the upcoming year. • Produced new corporate brochures.
Personnel	• Implemented and supervised a new computerized payroll system. • Responsible for downsizing a department in times of restraint ('81/'82). • Recruited new employees with an exceptional success rate.
Strategic Planning	• Developed a five year strategic plan for the corporation as a whole, and each major department. • Identified an unmet customer need and created a plan to fill it. • Set and achieved corporate goals and objectives on a consistent basis.
WORK EXPERIENCE	ABC Company — Title XYZ Incorporated — Title QRT Limited — Title BNM Company Ltd. — Title MKO Conglomerate — Title UIA International — Title
EDUCATION	Completed numerous business and management courses including: • labour relations • business ethics • economics • accounting • statistics • organizational behaviour
OTHER INTERESTS	Chess, gardening, photography, public speaking, and breeding dogs.

References Available Upon Request

Covering Letter

September 10, 1991

Mr. Roman Numbers
V.P. Finance
567 Company Ltd.
1 Numerical Ave.
City, Province
M8U 7Y7

Dear Mr. Numbers,

I am taking the liberty of sending you my résumé on the recommendation of a mutual friend, Mr. Peter Piper. He may have called you on my behalf.

I am a chartered accountant with over fifteen years experience in general accounting specializing in the retail industry. In my last position at 123 Company, I prepared monthly financial statements, annual budgets and forecasts, and performed on-going analysis of the retailing operation. The company had sales of $25 million annually.

I spearheaded the installation of a new computer system, which improved the reporting system, provided much easier access to information and allowed for quicker and better analysis. Mr. Piper felt that my experience may be of interest to your company. Please find further information on my background and accomplishments in the enclosed résumé.

I would appreciate the opportunity to discuss what I can contribute to your company further with you, and I will call you on September 15th in the hope that we may set up a mutually convenient time to meet.

Sincerely,

Ms. Job Seeker
(555) 123-4567

Broadcast Letter

May 3, 1991

Ms. R. U. Important
President and C.E.O.
ABC Bank of Canada
100 Money Street
City, Province Q2W 5G6

Dear Ms. Important,

I read with great interest your comments on the effect of ____ on the banking industry in the <u>Globe and Mail</u> on May 2nd. I thoroughly agree with your analysis of the consequences we will face.

I have had a successful career over the past two decades with leading international banks. I am now seeking a position with a Canadian organization in which my services can be utilized most effectively. I am very interested in becoming associated with your bank because of the outstanding reputation of the ABC Bank of Canada. I believe that my abilities can contribute to the bank's profitability and successful growth. I have a great deal to offer, particularly in the areas of:

- Credit management and policy formulation, as I was responsible for _____ .
- Loan restructuring, recoveries, and legal administration, as I was able to restructure ____ and recover an "unrecoverable" loan by ___ .
- International relations, as I accomplished _____ .

There are also other aspects of my background that will be of interest to you. With my extensive experience in banking, your bank will start earning an immediate return on its investment in me.

I believe that a personal discussion will be of mutual interest and benefit, therefore I will call you next week in the hope that you will be able to fit me into your busy schedule for a meeting at your earliest convenience.

Sincerely,

Ms. Hope T. Bank
(416) 443-8765

111 Park Lane, Big City, Province M7U 3W1

Job Advertisement

Chief Executive Officer

Our client, a Canadian privately-held company, is a major retail/wholesale distributor of basic consumer products generating close to a half-billion dollars in annual revenue. The business has enjoyed excellent growth and profitability throughout its history. Its brand name is well-known and highly respected in the industry. Products are sold through an extensive network of franchised retail and wholesale accounts.

The CEO will report to the Chairman of the Board of Directors and, after an initial period of familiarization with industry dynamics, staff, customers and suppliers, will become fully responsible for all aspects of corporate strategy, policy and day-to-day operations.

The scope of this challenge requires that candidates be able to demonstrate a successful history of managing, developing and expanding a profitable, significant independent business unit. Corporate functions are comparatively few and, accordingly, a hands-on, entrepreneurial and informal approach to managing is most appropriate. The successful candidate will be a dynamic conceptualizer with excellent management and leadership qualities.

This is an outstanding opportunity for an exceptional executive with experience in a high volume, low profit margin operation. Please respond in confidence quoting project 0000.

Mr. R. U. Ready
Consultant
Search Company
1 Hope Street
City, Province N8U 7B6

Responding To An Advertisement

Mr. R. U. Ready   May 20, 1991
Consultant
Search Company
1 Hope Street
City, Province N8U 7B6

Dear Mr. Ready,

RE: PROJECT 0000, CHIEF EXECUTIVE OFFICER

Your recent advertisement in the (*name of publication*) has prompted me to express my interest in the above position, since my background and experience matches your requirements to a remarkable degree as shown below:

YOUR REQUIREMENTS	MY QUALIFICATIONS
* Demonstrate a successful history of managing, developing and expanding	* 11 years experience of building a successful business within a major corporation.
* Profitable, significant and independent business unit	* Managed and significantly increased the profits and profitability of an independent business unit.
* Hands-on entrepreneurial and informal approach	* An accurate description of my style of management as those who know my work will attest.
* Dynamic conceptualizer, excellent management and leadership qualities	* My successes, both in building teams and businesses, strategic and business planning and execution, leads me to believe that I possess these qualities.

YOU ARE LOOKING FOR AN EXCEPTIONAL EXECUTIVE
I AM LOOKING FOR AN OUTSTANDING OPPORTUNITY!

There is much more about my background that I would like to share with you. Please find my résumé attached. I look forward to meeting you to discuss the company, its strategy and objectives. I look forward to hearing from you.

Sincerely,

Mr. Eager Beaver, M.B.A.
(676) 543-0987

Advice-Seeking/Information-Gathering Letter

A) *Career Change*

Name
Title
Company
Address
Postal Code

Date

Dear Mr. Big,

I am a successful business executive with ___ years experience in the ___ industry. I find myself at a crossroads in my career and I am considering a career change.

I am currently researching the ___ industry, and I would like to benefit from the experience and knowledge of successful, accomplished people in this field like yourself.

I would value the opportunity to have a brief meeting with you. I have several questions that I believe you could help me to clarify. My career is very important to me, and I want to make informed and proper decisions, and I trust that I would gain some valuable insight from your advice.

I will call you on ___ (month) ___ (day) to see if your schedule will permit a twenty minute meeting in the near future. I look forward to speaking with you. Thank you for considering my request.

Sincerely,

Mr. Job Seeker
(888) 354-9674

Advice Seeking/Information Gathering Letter (con't)

B) General

Name
Title
Company
Address
Postal Code

Date

Dear Ms. Successful Executive,

I am a successful business executive with ___ years experience in ___ industry. I am currently re-examining my career and future options.

Because my career is so important to me, I want to make the most informed, thought out and advantageous decisions possible. That is why I am seeking the advice of successful, accomplished people like yourself. I have always respected and admired your career and I hope to be able to benefit from your expertise and knowledge.

I wonder if you could meet with me, briefly, to assist me in my career decisions. I have several questions and options and I believe that you could shed some light on my dilemma.

I will call you on ___ (month) ___ (day) to see if your schedule will permit a twenty minute meeting in the near future. I look forward to speaking with you. Thank you for considering my request.

Sincerely,

Ms. Job Hunter
(887) 567-0987

A Blueprint For Success

How To Get What You Want

"You don't get what you deserve, you get what you negotiate."

—Unknown

Have you ever:

* talked yourself out of a traffic ticket?
* managed to secure a room in a hotel when the desk clerk told you there was no room available?
* got a good deal on a mortgage?
* bargained for a discount on a purchase?
* asked for a raise and got one?
* obtained a better deal from a supplier?
* disciplined children?
* been in any type of long-term relationship?

Well then, you know how to negotiate. Negotiation is really just simply the give and take of life, and life is a process of always trying to get what you want, while still keeping in the game (and, of course, not hurting anyone in the process). Negotiation is instinctual and intuitive. Even a two-year-old can negotiate. Does "Can I have one more cookie if I go to bed now?" sound familiar?

It is human nature to try to get what we want. The key to successful and lasting negotiation is for all parties involved in the negotiation to feel that their needs have been met and they have come out ahead. Not necessarily come out ahead of their "opponents," but rather emerge from the negotiation better off then they were when the process began. This is called a *win/win* co-operative situation.

Historically, people have thought that there is always a winner and a loser in transactions. If I got my needs met, that meant you had to have given up your needs and lost. That was called a *win/lose* competitive situation. Let's hope this type of thinking has gone the way of the dinosaur and is gone for good. If you enter a negotiation situation with a win/win philosophy and you don't try to triumph *over* your opponent by reaching your goals at the *expense* of their objectives, then you stand more of a chance of being successful.

People (or corporations) have many needs that they want fulfilled. Some needs may even be subconscious and unexpressed. Try to know what your opponant's real needs are. Understand their position.

> **"If there is one secret of success, it lies in the ability to get the other person's point of view and see things from that person's angle as well as from your own."**
> —HENRY FORD

Always enter any negotiation prepared. For example, when negotiating a compensation package for a new job, try to learn the needs of the company, industry standards, and what the company's reputation for remuneration is. You will also have different needs. Know clearly what you *must* or absolutely need to have in a negotiation; what you *want* or would like to have; and what you would be willing to *give up* before you enter any negotiation. Know and understand what you want and what you have, and what they want and what they have. Then look for creative ways to make it fit.

Don't think that just because you are out of work and have been offered a job (thank goodness) that you are powerless to negotiate. That is not true. *You* have been offered the job. That means they want *you*. They feel that you are the best person for the job; so make sure that you negotiate the best deal for you. Also, calmly, objectively, and skillfully negotiating for a good employment package (that is fair to both you and the company) will earn you your new employer's respect. They will consider how well you negotiate your own contract to be indicative of how well you will negotiate with your staff, your colleagues, your clients, your suppliers, and your boss.

By now you know the importance of rehearsing things before they take place, so be sure to role play the negotiation process with a friend and also run through the successful negotiation in your mind. Imagine the discussion in as much detail as possible. Know your options, have clear expectations, and remember that you have power. Then, when the negotiation actually takes place, you will be prepared. You will have a confident, positive attitude. Be open, creative, and flexible in the discussions, but don't lose sight of your goals. Always try to keep the relationship on a positive note. If you hit a snag that you can't agree on, let it go and come back to it later. Usually it will seem easier to work out after all the give and take of the other items.

> *"Let us begin anew, remembering on both sides that civility is not a sign of weakness, that sincerity is always subject to proof. Let us never negotiate out of fear. But let us never fear to negotiate."*
>
> —JOHN F. KENNEDY

There are four key aspects of negotiation:

1. *Information* — be sure to do your homework.

2. *Time Pressure* — try to find out what their deadline is (and is it etched in stone or flexible) and be aware of your own time constraints.

3. *Power* — whether real or perceived, understand their power dynamics, and make sure you enter into negotiations feeling not only worthwhile, but empowered!

4. *Communication* — how well you are able to communicate and understand their communication is integral to the negotiation process.

There are certain things to do, and not to do, that will help to achieve successful negotiations and avoid problems. Here is some negotiating advice.

Negotiation Tips

- Know the going-in position of all parties involved. Understand and agree on the problem to be solved, and where the issues currently stand.

- Don't come across as a know-it-all. That is an irritating posture. Ask questions — even when you think you know the answer. You may find out that you were wrong or better yet, get more information. At the very least you will get clarification.

- Listen, and I mean really listen and *hear* what is being said. Listen more than you talk. No one ever learned anything while talking.

- Establish an environment of candor and trust up front.

- Be positive. Create a comfortable, co-operative climate. Don't be abrasive or abusive. Try to avoid conflict and friction at all costs.

- Realistically and objectively analyze the other side's position. Challenge your assumptions. Know your options. Don't jump to conclusions.

- Be willing to take calculated risks. (Make sure you have solid reliable information before you take a big risk.)

- Don't be afraid of time. The more time that is spent negotiating, the more the other party will be willing to find a solution. ("I can't have wasted all this time for nothing! We must make this work.") Also, most concessions are made when a deadline is looming. (Another reason to know their *real* deadline.)

- As mentioned earlier, if a point of contention is reached, put it on the back burner and return to it later. The more chips you or the other party have cashed or thrown in may alter the perception of the contentious issue and should make an agreement easier to reach.

- Use the notion of precedent to your advantage ("We've always done it this way"); but don't be taken in by it ("Is it a necessity to do it this way just because it has always been done this way before? Why?").

- Understand your opponents *real* needs and try to fill them.

- Be pleasantly persistent.

- Get the involvement (time, money, energy) of the other party(s). They will be more willing to believe in something they helped to create.

- Don't tip your hand and show that you feel that you *must* have something. *Never* appear desperate.

- Understand the style of your adversaries and try to match it. For example, is the person you are negotiating with friendly, relaxed, and amiable, or are you facing a hard-driving, analytical person who is not at all interested in you, but only the facts?

- If faced with a complex issue that is bogging down the process, try to break up the issue into its smaller, simpler, easier-to-deal-with component parts.

- Watch your communication — your body language, your voice, and what you say, and that of your opponents. You can get (or inadvertently give) telling cues from physiology.

- If things are getting nowhere, if you've reached an impasse, or if things are starting to get out of hand, *stop*. Recognize when it is necessary to take a break. Don't push too hard.

- Understand that others may have different information or experiences than you have. Try to walk in their shoes. Always treat your opponent with respect and dignity. Tact and diplomacy are key to successful negotiations.

- Remember that for every action there is a reaction.
- Use your instincts and listen to your gut; yet don't lose sight of logic.
- Most of all, enjoy the process. It is like a game. Keep your eye on the ball, toss it around, recognize the fake outs, and try to score.

"I have no right to say or do anything that diminishes a man in his own eyes. What matters is not what I think of him, but what he thinks of himself. Hurting a man in his dignity is a crime."
—ANTOINE DE SAINT-EPPUPERY

It is important to remember that the desired outcome is a mutually beneficial agreement where that both (or all) parties feel that they have gained something and received a fair deal. Winning does *not* mean demolishing your opponent or gaining at their loss. Instead, a successful negotiation entails fulfilling your needs, while at the same time fulfilling the needs of your opponent. All sides *can* get what they want because no two people are the same. Everyone has their own set of needs, wants, desires, likes, and dislikes. The key is knowing what you want, what they want and creatively, openly, and flexibly filling those desires. Therefore, with a *win/win* attitude, you can negotiate anything and win!

YOU CAN GET WHAT YOU WANT!

"For fifty years we heard too much about the things which divided us. Let us now make a great effort to remember the things which unite us. With these links we can begin to forge a new and better understanding in the future."
—QUEEN ELIZABETH II

The Economic Picture For The Nineties

"The one unchangeable certainty is that noth-ing is unchangeable or certain."
—JOHN F. KENNEDY

The decade of the nineties is going to be in no way like the last decade — or any other decade that has come before. The boom years of the past are gone. We are undergoing a massive restructuring of our economy. The nineties will be a tough and turbulent period for business because they will be transitional years. (And you already know the "dis-comfort" of transition!) It will be a time of re-alignment and re-evaluation. Mostly, it will be a time of incredible change and competition.

There have been such extraordinary technological changes (especially in transportation and communica-tion) that people are no longer astonished at the over-whelming developments. For example, no one blinks twice at the fact that you can deposit money in a bank account in Hong Kong and have it recorded in Canada ten seconds later! We can simultaneously communicate to most coun-tries in the world! In fact, the label "foreign" correspond-ent has been dropped by CNN, because their signal goes into every country in the world that receives television. So, what then is "foreign"? Technologically, we've become a very small world. These changes will still continue and will persist at an accelerated pace.

"The world is moving so fast these days, that the man who says it can't be done is generally interrupted by someone doing it."
—HARRY EMERSON FOSDICK

The technological changes have been striking; but they didn't hit our hearts and souls like the institutional and social changes that have taken place over the past decade. For example:

- The frail state of the Russian economy and communism.

- Soviet President Mikhail Gorbachev asking to be included in the G7 for a broader participation in world economics.

- The unification of Germany.

- The movement of the European common market in 1992.

- And here at home, the signing of the bilateral free trade agreement between Canada and The United States (soon to include Mexico).

All these changes have been overwhelmingly important and they have occurred very fast.

The combination of these institutional and social changes with our technological capabilities has led to a world economic market. Today, business must operate and be able to compete in a global economy. As the walls around countries come down, borders become economically irrelevant. Companies can't hide themselves under a patriotic flag and expect to survive. Money has no heart, no soul, no conscience, and no homeland. Business will have to examine its costs against a world market and adjust itself accordingly. For example, if a company can run a plant in Mexico for a fraction of the cost that it can run it elsewhere, it may have no other choice but to move the plant to Mexico. Within that context, a lot of uprooting has and will continue to take place. A company can no longer decide to remain domestic and not think internationally, because if that company is not competitive, another company will come in and take away the domestic market from them. Businesses must think globally and be cost competitive. There is nowhere to hide and there is no choice.

"The graveyard of business is littered with companies that failed to recognize inevitable changes."

—ANONYMOUS

Companies must examine themselves closely and decide what business it is that they are really in, where they have a globally competitive advantage, and where they should be in a global context. Then they will have to restructure accordingly. An example of this concentration on what a company does well is the following: Procter and Gamble recently bought Facelle Royale from C. P. Forest Products. C. P. only had one plant producing Facelle products. They were not efficient. C. P. Forest was really in the pulp, hard paper, and newsprint business. They realized that they must specialize in what they are good at. They could no longer play in the towel/tissue game. It's not the core business they are in. They can be a world player in newsprint; but, they can't even be a predominant national player in the towel/tissue business. They have recognized that they must re-strategize what their business is in order to stay in business.

This process of restructuring (divesting, acquiring, etc.) in a global context will make the early nineties a very difficult period. Businesses that cannot compete in this new reality will fail (as we are already seeing far too often these days). As the world opens up, success benchmarks will also have to change. Businesses will be judged on world class standards. It isn't going to be a matter of whether the business did better than last year. It isn't going to be good enough to simply be good enough anymore. There will be no safety net. A dramatic example of a coalition that has been necessitated by the economy is the alliance of IBM with its former enemy, Apple Computer. They agreed to exchange technologies and jointly develop new machines in the hope that they will shape the direction of the industry, instead of losing their respective power and having to be shaped by the industry. In the face of new competition, market uncertainties, changing new technologies, and a shrinking world, even these computer giants have to adapt.

An interesting phenomenon is just as we are operating in larger economic units we find ourselves operating in smaller political units. The reaction to globalization is localization. Economic melding has led to an increased identification with smaller, localized interests and identities. There is a backlash against uniformity, and an increase in individualism. People want to assert their uniqueness. They no longer want to be part of the masses. For example:

- The Republics of Croatia and Slovania are fighting with Yugoslavian authorities.

- Afganistan rebelled against Communist rule.

- Individual Russian Republics are debating what kind of freedom they will have.

- In Canada, the province of Quebec is demanding to be recognized as a distinct society.

That means we will have to work better locally and globally. We must consider global economics and local cultures. That is a tough prescription. There will be an increased respect for and power of the individual in the nineties. The collective and mass marketing is out; and customization and target and niche marketing is in.

The changes that the nineties will bring will be traumatic, challenging, unpredictable, and unavoidable. It will be a time of re-thinking, re-alignment, re-evaluation, and re-structuring.

A Note On Canada

Canadian policy set by government has never been to foster competition. Rather, it has been to prevent it. Canada has always had a protectionist policy. One of the reasons that Canada is such a high cost country is due to the enormous monopolies that have been created by government. (For example, Canada is one of the last countries in the world where beer is still sold under monopoly conditions through the Brewers Retail Stores, therefore eliminating any price competition for the suds.) Another government policy in Canada has been to subsidize industries that were in trouble to keep employment high. For example, the steel industry has been heavily subsidized in Canada for years. That will no longer be a viable option and those companies that have enjoyed an influx of funds from the government will be in trouble. Subsidies have kept prices very high, and those prices must come back in line with the rest of the world. In fact, many plants in Canada have already shut down, and there will continue to be a migration of manufacturing jobs to the United States because those plants that are inefficient on an international scale will no longer be able to compete. The early nineties will be a time of a harsh shake-out, and the manufacturing sector will experience significant pressure. The days of isolation and protection are over.

Many Canadians are cross-border shopping in the U.S. This hot issue of civil disobedience is a reaction of Canadians to an astounding price differential. Costs *must* be competitive. Canadian retailers close to the U.S. border are finding this out the hard way, as consumers are shopping in the States in droves, where prices are much cheaper. There will continue to be a migration of retail sales from Canada to the U.S., until Canadians can pay comparable prices for goods and services in Canada. People will *only* pay a cost of convenience premium. Different people and different business sectors will have different convenience premiums. Canadian businesses must know the convenience cost people are willing to pay in their sector of the economy and bridge that gap in price. They must understand this in order to survive. Competition will be fierce and Canadian business will have to be less insular in their perspective. As the world becomes one marketplace, companies must rationalize. For example, five years ago, Canadian plants were making products for Canadian consumers. Now, Canadian plants are making products for North American consumers — or they are not making products at all.

There was a false sense of complacency in Canada, and, therefore Canada is not highly geared toward a global economy and must re-orient itself to be more effectively able to compete in the world-competitive nineties.

"It is a rare enterprise that can assume it will be serving exactly the same market with the same products in ten years time."

—JESSIE WERNER

The Changing Face Of Doing Business

"Business only contributes fully to society if it is efficient, successful, profitable and socially responsible."

—LORD SIEFF

There is a new and emerging respect and concern for the environment. Corporations will have to be concerned about being "green" as environmentalism becomes a key issue for consumers of the nineties. Business will also be more concerned about being good corporate citizens in all aspects of how they do business. The greed of the eighties will be replaced by concern for issues and a revival of business ethics.

Another big change that corporations will have to adapt to is a greater flexibility and mobility of its work force. The personal computer, fax machine, and new telephone capabilities will allow for an increased mobility of labour in the nineties. Working in one's home as part of a corporate set-up will be just as likely as working in an office environment. Work arrangements will be flexible. There will also be variations on the one-person-one-job philosophy. Instead, there will be an increase in part-time work, project work, contract work, job sharing arrangements, flex-time, and self-employment. Looking for another nest to lay your weary body and have job security is not realistic for the nineties.

The days of the traditional pyramid-style, unfriendly, us-versus-them style of management is gone. A flatter, leaner, friendlier organizational structure is in. There will be greater employee participation and appreciation, and, individual productivity and creativity will play a major role in company performance. There will be an emphasis on the process as well as the product. Quality, innovation, service, people, and product integrity will make companies stand out in the nineties. There will be less and less security in jobs and more of a project orientation taking over. The corporation cannot be relied upon to take care of its workers, and careers may be based on a series of projects in one or many companies. There will also be an increase in subcontracting as companies realize that "in-house" may not be the most efficient way to do business. Many facets of a company's operations can be handled faster, cheaper, and better by outside specialized service experts. Companies that share information and resources are able to respond quickly to change, think longer term, and constantly monitor the global external environment will succeed in the nineties.

"There is no security on this earth, there is only opportunity."
—General Douglas MacAuthur

Success Factors In The Nineties

"Success is not the result of spontaneous combustion. You must set yourself on fire."
—Reggie Leach

In the nineties, the job market will be tight, with the predominant number of new jobs being created by smaller companies. Even as the large corporations get larger and larger, the job availability in these corporations will still shrink, because as companies buy out others, synergies are created in overhead. One major source of overhead is staff. Therefore, corporations will be larger and leaner and net employment will be down. There will still be some hiring due to turnover, retirement, and new opportunities, but the competition for these jobs will be fierce. Due to the changing organizational structure, the skills that employers will be looking for in the nineties will be: the ability to: manage ambiguous networks, teams, and relationships; champion and embrace change; deal with uncertainty; take calculated risks; motivate and inspire others; be creative and proactive; and have the ability to make quick and good decisions. Employers will look for confident, enterprising, dependable, committed people, with foresight, vision, intuition, and sensitivity to lead them through the nineties.

Ironically, in this age of machines, you'll have to have good interpersonal and communication skills to succeed. With an aging and culturally mixed work force, there will be a demand for executives who can manage, relate to, and accommodate different work ethics and values. Executives must be able to think globally and know about not only their own country, but other countries as well. A broad understanding of the world around them will be as necessary as understanding the community they're in.

It will be very helpful to speak another language. If you are living in one country, and come from another and speak a native language, leverage your background. Play up the fact that you've got cultural and language skills from another country. With the world becoming smaller, companies will look for executives who are comfortable in a foreign language and culture to take advantage of opportunities in unfamiliar settings. In fact, being able to manage abroad is key expertise that will be required in the nineties. If you have the chance to work overseas, take it. Learn how to operate in a foreign market, and understand the differences that exist between competing in different countries such as, the United States, Canada, Europe, and the Far East. That broader global perspective will be a major success factor in the nineties.

The nineties will be a time of incredible change (innovation, greater international competition, and lightening-speed technological advancements). But the fact of the matter is, people generally don't like change. It is uncomfortable. Many people would rather stay with something they hate, rather than risk changing and trying something new. (Not you any more — right?!)

> *"When faced with the choice between changing and proving there's no need to do so, most people get busy on the proof."*
> —JOHN KENNETH GALBRAITH

You can't get too comfortable with or attached to what worked in the past. It is a different ball game now. Don't rely on the old, "If it ain't broke, don't fix it" philosophy because, in the face of this environment, by the time people recognize that it's broken, it is too late to fix it. Be prepared to take risks. If you don't risk making a big mistake, you won't be able to take a big leap forward.

> *"Before you can hit a jackpot, you have to put a coin in the machine."*
> —FLIP WILSON

If you don't feel nervous, you're only maintaining the status quo. That will get you nowhere in the nineties. So get comfortable with change. You've learned how to deal with and cope with change as you've gone through this book, with regard to your job loss. Now, take those skills and be a manager of change. Most people can only talk about change management. You have lived it, so parlay that into a skill you can take to your next opportunity.

Adaptation and flexibility will be key skills for success in the nineties. It won't be good enough to simply learn a skill once and build your career on replicating it, or even upgrading it. You may have to learn a series of different skills and operate in a series of different milieus. Chances are you will have to change not only your job, but the type of work that you do a few times over the course of your career. In fact, executives can expect to get fired at *least* once in their careers. So, looked at in that perspective, everyone will have to go through job loss at some time or another. You have a head start. Aren't you lucky? No one will be immune to these coming changes. They are the virus of the nineties. You can inoculate yourself by preparing for these circumstances. Be adaptable, flexible, and creative when defining your new career goals. Be a generalist who is able to take your skills and adapt them to many situations. Always continue to be a student. Read business magazines, keep up with the latest knowledge and technology. Networking, volunteer work, and just being involved and visible in your next company and in your community will be very important, as you should always be on the lookout for new job opportunities (as security will be a thing of the past). You can't wait for the tide of employment to come in and suck everyone up and carry you with it. You'll be waiting a very, very long time!

> *"One must never lose time in vainly regretting the past nor in complaining about the changes which cause us discomfort, for change is the very essence of life."*
> —ANATOLE FRANCE

Tips For Operating In The Nineties

Realistically assess the future growth (or decline) potential of the business sector you were in. Don't try to re-position yourself in a declining job sector. You may get lucky, but you'll be fighting an uphill battle. Instead, redefine what you'd like to do and prepare yourself for re-entry into another area. Many jobs that have been lost are not coming back, so be aware of your options.

Here Are Some Suggestions

- Visit a foreign country and look for trade opportunities. Look for products to import, or become an expert at how to take businesses into that country and set them up, and sell that expertise to companies who want to expand globally.

- Learn another language. That will definitely be an advantage in the competitive job market of the nineties.

- Look for work in companies that are either mammoth and international in scope, or serve a market niche.

- The service industry will be a growth sector in the nineties.

- Environmentally-oriented businesses will flourish (waste-management, etc.) so you may want to look for work in that sector.

It will take courage, self-knowledge, a feeling of empowerment, and a desire to control your own destiny to be successful in the nineties. Look for that light at the end of the tunnel and ask yourself, "Do I want that light to be a train coming at me, or do I want that light to be some sort of inspiration?" It's up to you.

The Only Thing To Fear Is Fear Itself

"Fear is that little darkroom where negatives are developed."
—MICHAEL PRITCHARD

Fear. Yuck. What an awful feeling. Or is it? All fear is, is your body getting ready to fight or flee. It is a state of arousal and excitement. That's all. Next time you feel fear, label it excitement and you'll have a new outlook on that which you fear. There are generally four components of fear. Let's look at them in a new light.

1. **FEAR Of PAIN**. Pain is a great motivator. Many people are spurred on to great successes only after hitting rock bottom and enduring the pain and saying, "That's it! I've had enough! I'm going to do something about it!" If life was more comfortable for many of these people, they wouldn't have been motivated to kick-start themselves to achieve greatness. Let pain motivate you and drive you on to achieve great things in your life. For example, Lee Iacocca was fired from Ford. As C.E.O of Chrysler, he is now thought of as one of the most recognized, powerful, and respected businessmen today. The pain he experienced from being fired at Ford spurred him on to accept a challenge at Chrysler that he may not otherwise have taken.

2. **FEAR OF THE UNKNOWN**. If you are afraid of what *may* happen, you are inhibited from taking action. In order to be successful, you must do things, take action, and work towards your goals. So break through that limiting fear and do what it is you fear.

"Do the thing you fear and the death of fear is certain."

—EMERSON

That is a very liberating feeling. You must have faith that your world and life as we know it won't be destroyed (in fact, it will usually be better) if you confront your fear of the unknown and just do it. The funny thing about fears is that when you confront them, they are never even half as bad or as scary as you had imagined.

"You gain strength, courage and confidence by every experience in which you really stop to look fear in the face. You are able to say to yourself, 'I lived through this horror. I can take the next thing that comes along.' You must do the thing you think you cannot do."

—ELEANOR ROOSEVELT

3. **FEAR OF REJECTION**. So you get turned down for a job. So what? It will allow a better opportunity to come along, or force you to make a better situation for yourself. For example, did you know that Tom Watson was fired from NCR, so he started a little company called IBM. Have you ever heard of it?! Boris Yeltsin was expelled from the communist party that he belonged to, and was publicly maligned in the press. He went on to become the first elected President of the Russian Republic.

   Have you ever really wanted to ask someone out but didn't because you were afraid that they'd say *no*? The word "no" can't hurt you if you don't let it. So what if that person says no? They are making room in your life for the right person. Yet, what if that person is *the* one for you and would have said *yes*?! Look at what you lost out on — just because you were afraid of a little two letter word. Seems silly doesn't it? What opportunities have you lost out on because you were afraid of being rejected? You won't let that happen again, will you?! Even if the worst happens, you get rejected and it hurts, in fact it's a little painful, well, that's great! Why? Because pain motivates you. Right?

4. **FEAR OF FAILURE**. First of all, you can never fail. That's right. Never. Each time you try something and it doesn't work, that is not a failure; it is a *result* of your actions. If it is not the outcome you had wanted, then, you *learned* how to not do something. Setbacks are the necessary feedback you need to learn how to do something successfully. Everyone makes mistakes. They are the best teachers. Haven't you learned more from your mistakes than from your successes? When you have a great success, you go off and celebrate. When you have a great "failure" you stop and think about what went wrong, how to change it, and do it better. Setbacks, frustrations, and failures are all just part of learning. Turn those

stumbling blocks into stepping stones. All great successes have a trail of failed attempts, mistakes, and frustrations in their wake. So don't be hard on yourself. You succeed by learning and you learn by doing.

"We learn wisdom from failure much more than from success; we often discover what will do, by finding out what will not do; and probably he who never made a mistake never made a discovery."

—SAMUEL SMILES

Eddie Arcaro lost his first forty-five races before he later became known as one of the greatest jockeys of all time. Hank Aaron struck out almost twice as often as he hit a home run. Napoleon lost one-third of all the important battles he fought, but he is remembered for his astounding victories.

"Far better it is to dare mighty things, to win glorious triumphs even though checkered by failure, than to rank with those poor spirits who neither enjoy nor suffer much because they live in the gray twilight that knows neither victory nor defeat."

—THEODORE ROOSEVELT

Did you know that when Kleenex first came out on the market it was a total failure? The makers of Kleenex originally pitched it as a paper face cloth. It bombed. Then they discovered that people were using Kleenex as a disposable handkerchief. They recognized this, changed their pitch, marketed Kleenex as a disposable handkerchief and the rest is history. Are you familiar with those handy Post-It Notes? I'm sure that you've used them a million times. Are you aware that the chemist at 3M was trying to make a super-adhesive, one that would stick forever, when he "failed" and instead made a temporary adhesive. Instead of seeing that as a failure, he looked for an opportunity and discovered a new use for that new adhesive technology and Post-It Notes were made!

"The greatest mistake a man can make is to be afraid of making one."

—ELBERT HUBBARD

As long as you keep trying and always do your very best, you are succeeding. The key is to be flexible. If you aren't getting the result you desire, recognize it as an outcome — not a failure — learn from it, alter your behaviour and try again. Think of your failures as a radar device on an airplane. It lets you know when you are off course and signals you to alter your direction to keep you on the right track towards where you want to go. You must take risks to grow and fulfill your dreams. Playing it safe never made anyone successful. Use the pain, failure, rejection, fear, difficulties, and tragedies in your life to learn. And then go on. If you triumph over your fears you break through the limitations on your life!

"To conquer fear is the beginning of wisdom."

—BERTRAND RUSSELL

Today Is Your Most Prized Possession

Before you can move on with your life, you've got to let go of your resentment, anger, guilt, and sorrow over the past.

"To be wronged or robbed is nothing unless you continue to remember it."

—CONFUCIUS

What's done is done. Yesterday ended last night and it is gone forever. There is nothing you can do to bring it back, or change what has already happened. All you can do is learn from it and then forget it. Don't waste valuable time and energy over yesterday's events or mistakes. Forgive others and forgive yourself. Then you will be able to move on. Enjoy today. Live each day to the fullest because when it is over it is gone forever and can never be re-lived.

> *"Think that this day will never dawn again."*
> —DANTE

Don't darken the present with regrets from the past or with fear of the future. Worrying about what happened yesterday or last year, or what could happen tomorrow or next year, just takes the pleasure out of the present.

> *"Yesterday is a cancelled check; tomorrow is a promissory note; today is the only cash you have — so spend it wisely."*
> —KAY LYONS

Worry and resentment take energy and tire you out. Instead use that energy and live each day to its fullest with passion and enthusiasm.

> *"The real secret of success is enthusiasm."*
> —WALTER CHRYSLER

Enjoy life one day at a time. Don't put off living, as many who are dying can tell you. It is interesting that people who come close to death often have a new lease and outlook on life. They know first hand how precious life is, and they are able to "not sweat the small stuff" and they have realized that "it is all small stuff." Don't wait until you nearly lose your life to be able to appreciate how precious each day is.

You only have one life (or at least one that you can consciously remember — this is not the place to debate after-life or re-incarnation), and time slips away very fast, so don't waste your life away worrying, dreading, wishing, or regretting. Spend your life living and enjoying and being happy. Think about what you have to be grateful for.

Then rejoice in that. Don't dwell on what you don't have and be resentful or bitter.

"We seldom think of what we have but always of what we lack."

—Schapenhauer

As the old saying goes, "Today is the first day of the rest of your life." Use it well. Think of your life as a do-it-yourself project. It will be what you make it.

Humour — Never Leave Home Without It!

A great friend and companion to go through life with is humour. If you are able to laugh at yourself, and to laugh at life you will be infinitely less stressed and able to find happiness wherever you go. Adjust to the ups and downs in life by trying to see the humour in any situation. If you look hard enough, there usually is a funny side to all experiences. Haven't you ever said to yourself, "Someday I'll look back on this and laugh"? Why wait? Alleviate some of the stress of the situation and laugh now. You'll feel *so* much better. Humour is also the best ice-breaker and tension reliever that there is. When you find yourself in a tense or new situation, try to inject some humour and those around you will be appreciative and you will feel better too. Don't take yourself or life too seriously. Lighten up. Don't carry such a heavy load.

Have fun and enjoy life to its fullest!

You Can Do It!

Yes you can. Never forget that. Your life is the way it is because of the choices you make and the attitudes you have. Your future is up to you.

"We make our fortunes and call them fate."

—Benjamin Disraeli

You must believe in yourself and in your dreams. You can do whatever it is you set your mind on doing. It will take commitment, diligence, imagination, persistence, discipline, hard work, and a strong belief that you can do it.

"The man who wins may have been counted out several times, but he didn't hear the referee."

—H. E. JANSEN

Never give up on your dreams. Sylvester Stallone had his dream rejected by others over one thousand times! He never let his dream die and ended up making his dream — Rocky — come true. (Again and again, in fact!)

"The future belongs to those who believe in the beauty of their dreams."

—ELEANOR ROOSEVELT

Fred Smith went to Yale business school. He did his thesis proposing a courier service concept. He got a "C" grade. His professors thought the idea of a courier service — when there is a perfectly fine mail system — was ludicrous! That didn't deter determined Fred. When he graduated he invested his life savings in his "ludicrous" concept and Federal Express was in business. It is now a billion dollar a year business.

"Whatever you can do, or dream you can . . . begin it. Boldness has genius, power and magic in it."

—GOETHE

It is never too late to pursue your dreams. Ray Kroc, the founder of McDonalds didn't "make it" until he was well into his fifties. He was a paper cup salesman for seventeen years. Then he took a risk and struck out on his own in the milkshake machine business. In his travels he met the McDonald brothers and was very impressed by their ability to make many milkshakes simultaneously.

That gave Ray Kroc an idea. He had a vision for assembly-line food. He never gave up on his dream and built McDonalds into a multi-billion dollar world-wide business. Always pursue your dreams. Visualize them coming true. See them, hear them, feel them, and make them real.

> *"I know of no more encouraging fact than the unquestionable ability of man to elevate his life by a conscious endeavor... if one advances confidently in the direction of his dreams, and endeavors to live the life he has imagined, he will meet with a success unexpected in common hours."*
>
> —HENRY DAVID THOREAU

You are stronger than you realize. You have an inner strength that is able to endure anything that life throws your way. In times of difficulty, pull out what is already inside of you.

> *"There is no birth of consciousness without pain."*
>
> —C.G. YUNG

Here is how Paul T. had to really face the tragedies in life and how he pulled himself through:

"I had worked at a major soft drink company for fifteen years right out of college. Actually, I started at that company while I was still in college working on a truck. I built my whole career at that company and I worked my way up to the level of Senior Vice-President of Marketing and Sales. About four years ago we had an opportunity to buy the company. We were running a strong operation and therefore they felt the best people to sell it to would be the management group already in place. I was part of that group. Leading our team was our President, Jordan. Jordan was a superb person and my best friend. In an effort to purchase the company, we borrowed the money and went to see our lawyer, Ted, and he helped us put the deal together. He introduced us to another guy, Bill, who came up with the balance of the equity capital needed. Ted and Bill told us the money was from Hong Kong. The bank did the deal and when all was said and done we owned a sixty million dollar company. We were on top of the world!

"Then my world collapsed. Six weeks later, Jordan got sick. He had lung cancer. At the same time, my mother was in the hospital with pancreatic cancer. I spent my time going back and forth between the two hospitals. Also at this time, my wife left me. We separated about one month before the business deal was signed. We had been married twelve years and had an eight-month-old daughter, who was the apple of my eye. Her mother took her.

"Jordan died very quickly. It killed me that he never really got to live his dream come true: He didn't get to run our company. After his death the management team was at a loss for a leader. We didn't know who to appoint. The lawyer who did the deal, Ted, suggested that he was the best person to take over that job. I personally didn't like Ted, but my partners thought it was a good idea, so we hired him. I became very unhappy there. I did not like, trust, or respect Ted. He was aware of my feelings, as I did nothing to hide them. I started to be pushed aside and became less and less involved in the day-to-day operations of *my* company. My relationship with Ted was deteriorating daily. He wanted to remove me. I was being shunted and kept from management meetings in a company I built!

"I was deeply troubled. On top of all the trouble at work, my mother was very ill and soon died, and my marriage was on the rocks and my daughter was gone and living with her mother. My whole world seemed totally black. I started to wonder why I should even bother to get up in the mornings. Then one day, the management team discovered that Ted wasn't honest with us when he was representing us as our lawyer. The equity capital raised by 'Hong Kong' investors was a front for Ted and his partner Bill. Therefore, we were not receiving good, objective representation because it turned out that our lawyer was really our partner! The management group (myself and the two others) decided to fire Ted for breach of trust. He ended up getting back in command (a long story) and promptly fired us!

"So there I was, after all those years with the company *gone*. I wasn't even offered any severance. I had no money (I gave what I had to my soon-to-be ex-wife), and litigation would take years. I had no job, my mother had just died, my best friend had recently died, and I just lost my wife and daughter. I also had huge staggering bills in front of me. A friend put me up in his basement. I lived out of a pull-out couch and boxes. Then I had to look for a job. It's funny, while you are working, everybody in the world is your friend and they all want to know you. When you don't have a job, nobody wants to have anything to do with you. It's like all of a sudden you have leprosy. Emotionally it is devastating. I felt like I had lost everything. It was a horrible, traumatic time. I couldn't even take my daughter for the weekend because I didn't really have a proper place to live. I didn't even have a car because they took away my BMW. They took away everything. I felt like I had nothing at all. Only my unemployment insurance cheques. I had no idea until I was unemployed how things that I'd always taken for granted, like health insurance, a car, car insurance, leases and the like are needed. I was terrified that I would not be able to provide for my daughter's future. My life was a mess.

"I realized that I couldn't continue on like that, so I reached deep down inside of myself, and collected all my strength and picked myself up and embarked on a job search campaign. I put together a résumé and sent it out, and I made many phone calls. Everyone was very nice, but no one had a job for me. Months later, I answered an advertisement in the newspaper for a Vice-President for a pet food/supply company. I went through the interview process and got the job. I had to move to another city. The job was great; but the commuting to see my daughter was horrendous. A few months later, I got a call from one of the old members of the management team. He was Vice-President of Operations at a small beverage company back in town. He put me in touch with the owner of that company, and after talking for a month, I was offered the job of Senior Vice-President of Sales and Marketing. This job is a wonderful challenge, because I am in a position of helping to build up this company. I am making the same money and enjoy the same perks that I had in my old job, and I am doing what I love! Another, very important up-side to this whole experience is that I met someone very special. When I got the job out of town, I had to negotiate a lease for another car. The woman who leased me my car is now the woman I love. I am very happy now. I am madly in love, I have a great job, and I get to see my daughter often.

"Then it hit me — I realized that I was going to be fine. I got through it. Looking back, it is hard to believe that at the beginning of that year, I had a happy marriage, a loving, healthy mother, an incredible best friend, and an exciting, fulfilling job. Before the year was out I lost it all. It was an emotional nightmare. It seemed that each day was worse than the next. For so long, my world was totally black and upside-down. I never thought I'd see daylight again. My friends helped me to get through this awful time. My *real* friends, who liked me for me; not for the power and prestige that my job gave me.

"It took a devastating experience for me to really take a good look at myself and figure out who I really am as a person. For so long I wasn't able to separate myself from my job. Now I know that a job may not always be there, but I will always be there for myself. I am glad to know myself better. I also know who my true friends are and I know that they will be there for me no matter what. It was hard, but I'll tell you, I am a nicer person because of it. I lost huge amounts of my (oversized) ego, but most importantly, I know now that my job is not me and if I ever lose my job again I'll survive."

*"We don't receive wisdom; we must discover it
for ourselves, after a journey that no one can
take for us or spare us."*

—MARCEL PROUST

So, next time you think you've got overwhelming problems, think back to Paul's story and I think that you'll feel better. Don't let the tragedies of life keep you down. Keep believing in yourself.

"Fall seven times, stand up eight."

—JAPANESE PROVERB

Joan Rivers personifies this message. She has suffered crushing defeats in her career and her personal life (especially when her husband committed suicide), all of which were reported with great relish by the gossip mongers, so her problems were made public for all to see. Yet through it all, she never lost her sense of humour and her belief in herself. She always picked herself up and tried again; and she now is the host of a very successful daytime talk show. She never gave up.

*"Perseverance is a great element of success.
If you only knock long enough and loud
enough at the gate, you are sure to wake
up somebody."*

—LONGFELLOW

Here is another example of how a steadfast belief in yourself — even in the face of discouragement and disbelief — can make your dream come true. This is the story of Donny Osmond, who went from child superstar to teen idol to obscurity. This is the story of his fight to come back:

"The 'Donny and Marie Show' was successful for awhile. Then they started to change the format of the show and tried to push us into things we did not really want to do. Both Marie and I were tired of the show and she wanted to move on and pursue her country music, and I wanted get going with my pop music. I was twenty years old when the show ended. Marie enjoyed quite a bit of success with her country music career, but it was much more difficult for me in the rock and roll scene.

"I started going back into the studio and doing demos and getting my name back out into the right circles. Basically, I had to start all over from scratch. I realized that it was going to be a very difficult transition because nobody that I can think of (with the exception of Michael Jackson) has been able to come back from being a teen idol to a legitimate adult performer. I realized that it just wasn't the public's perception that I had to change; I had to change the industry's perception of me as well. Yet, I was told by promotion managers and producers (actually anybody that I spoke to) that it was just not going to happen for me. Every door was slammed in my face!

"But I *knew* that I had the talent and I believed that in time and with a lot of perseverance I would come back. I was aware that the responsibility for getting my career back on track rested squarely on my shoulders. By going around town, doing demos, singing on other people's records I began to get a reputation that stood on my talent alone. There is a certain circle of people that are very influential in the music industry. I tried to get my name included in their conversations. Then I got my first big break. I got offered a part on Jeff Beck's upcoming album. They sent me the tape and they highlighted on the lyrics sheet exactly what I was supposed to sing. I realized how important this was for me, so rest assured, all night long I was practicing those lines — and *only* those lines. Well, I got to the studio the next day, and they said, 'Okay Donny, it's your turn. Go for it. Oh, by the way, you're not singing that part any more, instead you're to sing this new part.' I nearly died. That was a real test. It was unrehearsed and so my raw talent had to come through for me. It did. Now I finally had the industry on my side. Then, the public liked what they heard. My next big break happened when Peter Gabriel and I happened to be on the same show. We got to talking, he had heard about my talent and we decided to work together. I was back.

"It was a difficult struggle. Three ingredients helped me to keep going and to cope: my faith, which kept me mentally strong; my family, who gave me much needed moral support; and my belief in myself and my talent. I have not yet made it to the height of my expectations, but I think that people always should dream higher than what reality seems to be giving them at the moment. Reach high and expect to get there. I believe that life is built on cycles. Everything is cyclical. No matter what business you are in, no matter what age you're at, expect things to go up and down. There are peaks and valleys in life. Maybe other people's peaks and valleys aren't as extreme, but in the business of show business things are exaggerated and really up or really down. It is just part of the business. I'm happy now; but I will continue to reach higher and higher.

"Unfortunately, we live in a world of negativism. Most people will tell you that if you attempt something big you will fail. The advice they will give you is to give up. Forget it. I see things very differently. I believe that you can accomplish anything you want (within the realm of reality). Believe in yourself, know where your talents lie, work hard and cultivate your talents, and go for it."

~

"A great pleasure in life is doing what people say you cannot do."

— WALTER GOGEHOT

A Final Word

"Have no fear of perfection — you'll never reach it."

— SALVADORE DALI

Invest in your own knowledge and personal development. Don't expect unrealistic perfection in yourself or in others. Everyone is human. Always remember what you've been through. If you come across someone down the road that you are in a position to help, don't forget how much kindness and assistance can mean to someone who is down. Repay the kindness that you received . . . pass it on. You help yourself when you help others.

The success of life can only be measured by the degree of happiness you reach. Not by anyone else's standards. And everyone should choose their own road to find that happiness.

"Happiness? A good cigar, a good meal, and a good woman — or a bad woman. It depends on how much happiness you can handle."

— GEORGE BURNS

"Most people want to find happiness, but you don't find happiness any more than you find steel. You refine steel from rough ore and you fashion happiness from life's opportunities."

— CHARLES TEMPLETON

Accept what happens to you and look for the opportunities in every situation that life throws your way. Luck is recognizing when preparation meets opportunity. Don't let opportunities in disguise slip by you. Prepare for and expect success.

"What seems nasty, painful, evil, can become a source of beauty, joy and strength, if faced

with an open mind. Every moment is a golden one for him who has the vision to recognize it as such."

— HENRY MILLER

Believe in yourself. You can triumph over anything life sends your way. But you must take an active role. You can't win in the game of life, if you are not on the playing field. Spectators don't make a difference in this world. You've got to ride the waves and jump into the ocean of life by taking chances and having faith in yourself. Nothing is impossible!

YOU CAN DO IT!

"To laugh often and much; to win the respect of intelligent people and the affection of children; to earn the appreciation of honest critics and endure the betrayal of false friends; to appreciate beauty; to find the best in others; to leave the world a bit better, whether by a healthy child, a garden patch or a redeemed social condition; to know even one life has breathed easier because you have lived. This is to have succeeded."

—RALPH WALDO EMERSON